From Enoch To You

with Love

**What's Ahead, Why,
and How to Reach Safety**

Let these books which I have given you
be for an inheritance of Peace.
Hand them out to all who want them
and instruct them so they may see
God's very great and marvellous works.

(2 En.54:1,2)

Distribute into all your generations, and amongst the nations who shall have the sense to fear God, let them receive the books, and may they come to love them more than any food or earthly sweets, and read them and apply themselves to them; that all may hear from My face what is told them by you, that they may read and understand how there is no other God but me. And that they may always keep my commandments.

(En.36:1-2; 48:5-6)

What Readers are Saying

Joye, I love it! So well put together.

Joye has skilfully woven the book of Enoch (written before the flood of Noah and preserved by scribes through the generations) with Bible verses to give an up to date modern commentary which reads like today's newspaper.

As I read *From Enoch to You with Love* I was reminded that when I was in Qumran, Israel, I observed fragments of the book of Enoch carefully recorded and preserved by the Essenes. Some fragments were scribed up to 400 years before the birth of Yeshua. The discovery of these fragments confirmed the book of Enoch was very much part of the Essenes' search for the Messiah they were expecting. A guide at the Qumran site told us, "The Essenes disappeared in the first century and no one knows why". I felt like shouting, "It's because they found the Messiah they were looking for!"

Many are searching in these times for a pure gospel message. Joye has given us this message in *From*

Enoch to You with Love, skilfully using the writings of Enoch as the Essenes did on their journey to discover Messiah.

I am excited to recommend this book to you, and I know it will stir your hearts in your own search for Messiah as history unfolds before us.

Ian Johnson, His Amazing Glory Ministries

I am enjoying this book so much; it is so encouraging. The more I read the more I want to read and the more I get out of it. I've written notes but really, it's just so packed full of pearls and treasures. It's uplifting and anchoring and encouraging and inspiring all at the same time. I just love the part where you talk about house prayer meetings and our children and them having insight. And I love where Enoch describes the vision he had of the Flood and how his grandfather told him to pray for a remnant to be saved. There's so much in it I really, really love.

Virginia West, Worship Leader

Joye, your work is very clear and easy to read, although the information is deep and insightful. I find the Book of Enoch quite a scary concept to get my head around, and you have explained it lyrically and powerfully. I'm so glad you were able to write this.

Meredith Swift, Author: *Hearing His Voice*

From Enoch to You with Love –
What's Ahead, Why, and How to Reach Safety

© Joye Knauf Alit 2021
Jubilaté Publications.
Queensland, Australia.
joyealit@gmail.com

ISBN:978-0-9945736-2-9

Credits:
Cover Design: Beckon Creative
Image credits: Drawing by Frans Pourbus, photographed by Sailko. Creative Commons Attribution 3.0 Unported, https://creativecommons.org/licenses/by/3.0/deed.en. Storm 3827167. KevinCardin/Lightstock - Noah's Ark
Cover photos: Caleb Trevatt
Portraits: Alicia T DeZine Photography
Genealogy Map: Charles Palmquist

 A catalogue record for this book is available from the National Library of Australia.

"I take no pleasure in the death of anyone," declares the Sovereign Lord. "Turn away from all your offenses. Repent and live! Why will you die?"

(Ez.18:22,32)

From Enoch To You

with Love

What's Ahead, Why, and How to Reach Safety

Joye Knauf Alit

Dedication

I dedicate this book to the King Who
commissioned it
To Enoch and Heaven's crowd cheering us on
and to all those this blessing is addressed to
especially my family natural and spiritual
Pasifika, Asian and Global
Make Good Choices
Be Blessed

Table of Contents

God is coming to take His
creation back.

He's dealing with the evil that gets
between us.

Things to Know Before Beginning

The Books of Enoch are a miracle. Handle them with awe. Enoch is the first ever author and prophet that we know of. He recorded this ancient knowledge and was told to address it to *a generation far in the future*. Enoch, was writing when Adam was still around – about 800 years after creation, before time had clocked its first millennium. And about 800 years before the Great Flood of Noah's time.[1]

At the other end of the era (more than 5 millennia later!) something awesome has taken place. God has stepped in to fulfil His word to Enoch: *Then at the conclusion of that generation the books in your handwriting will be revealed, and those of your fathers,*

---

1   800AA - After Adam, or AM, Anno Mundi, Year of the World. Dates in this book are based on the Masoretic text of the Torah.

and the earthly guardians [of these books] will show them to the Men of Faith. And they will be recounted to that generation, and they will be glorified in the end more than in the beginning (2 En.35:1-3).

God commissioned the writing and oversaw the delivery of Enoch's books. He appointed men and nations and angels enroute to bring them safely through the Great Flood, the wanderings and wars and calamities of history, and the opposition of councils and cultures, to reach us at the set time. It is God's blessing to you through Enoch. Accept it with holy awe.

God's Backups

We no longer have scrolls in Enoch's handwriting, but God had back-up systems to save the data. Eventually a whole scribing industry evolved – a human printing press, meticulously copying and distributing the manuscripts as broadly as the nations. [I have great admiration for these dedicated men. Their solemn task was to exactly copy holy documents, without missing 'jot or tittle'.[2]]

His other backup was the children. They were taught, and memorized, holy writings from an early age.[3]

---

2   Tiny distinguishing marks in Hebrew writing.
3   We could learn a lot from their education system!

So when manuscripts became scarce over the centuries, the precious words, memorized and recorded ('inscribed indelibly') on hearts, would be carefully written down again.

Lost Data Retrieved and Redistributed

Called the 'Lost Book of the Bible', Enoch was 'lost' for 1000 years, after the Council of Laodicea in the 4th century, failed to approve it for the canon of scripture (along with John's Revelation! which didn't fit some of their current doctrines).[4]

The oldest known complete manuscripts of the books of Enoch (copied in the early 15th century AD) came from Ethiopia in their Ge'ez language. Enoch still forms part of the Ethiopian scripture canon today as it does also the Slavonic Bible.

Our early English translations come from this Ethiopian manuscript which reached Europe in the late 1700's and was first translated by R. Laurence in 1821. In 1912 R.H. Charles produced an updated translation based on Laurence but with access to more sources. Charles' version became the standard text. Now, more books and fragments of Enoch - in Greek, Aramaic, Coptic, Latin and more - are being discovered, hidden along with Scriptures and other

---

4   Wikipedia has good information on canon, manuscripts, translations, etc.

precious manuscripts in the Qumran Caves and other Judean desert sites. Seven copies in Aramaic were found, positively dated back to 300BC.[5] (That's over 2000 years old.) These findings verify the accuracy of the Ethiopian manuscripts and greatly help modern translators.

Nuts n Bolts

Sources Used in this Book. Direct Enoch quotes (in blue) throughout this work are downloaded from the public domain, RH Charles translation. I have at times condensed wordy text and modernized words. Lengthy passages that I have paraphrased are not printed in blue or treated as quotes.

I have used Rabbi Trimm, Lumpkin and Fickess (listed below), to compare texts, and on occasion may have used a translation from one of these if it was significant.

Access:

Online. You can access free copies of Enoch's books online. The free versions mainly use the 1912 translation by R.H.Charles. Here are some websites:

- *https://en.wikisource.org/wiki/The_Book_of_Enoch_(Charles)*

---

5   Milik – The Books of Enoch – Aramaic Fragments of Qumran Cave 4, Clarendon Press, Oxford, 1976

- *//bibleprophecyandtruth.com/notes/ theBookOfEnoch*
- *The Wesley Center online: Book of Enoch (the site I used for most quotes) //read. thebookofenoch.info/tboe.pdf*

In Print. Recently a flurry of Enoch translations and commentaries are coming off the press, part of God's delivery and distribution plan. I recommend getting a modern English translation (rather than the old, R.H. Charles one).

For an easy read I suggest:
Michael Fickess, 2014, *Enoch's Blessings,* Morningstar Publications, a paraphrase of most of Book 1.

For a more studious work:
Rabbi James Scott Trimm, 2017, *The Book of Enoch Study Edition, WNAE* - adds Jewish insights and comparative texts.
Joseph B. Lumpkin, 2011, *The Books of Enoch – The Angels, The Watchers and The Nephilim (With Extensive Commentary...)* Fifth Estate, AL.

Other respected, recent translators are:
M.A. Knibb 1978, *The Ethiopic Book of Enoch: A New Edition in the Light of the Aramaic Dead Sea Fragments,* Oxford Press.

George W.E. Nickelsburg, 2012, *1 Enoch: The Hermeneia Translation*, Fortress Press, Minneapolis. This work claims to consult 50 of the 90 available manuscripts plus Greek, Aramaic, Coptic and Latin fragments of the book.

I suggest you research the background of the translator. Some are professional academics for whom it is merely an academic exercise or debate. Some are drawn to its mystic knowledge. Find a faith-based translator who believes the books to have spiritual and prophetic importance.

Lumpkin[6] believes that New Testament writers (who accepted the Books of Enoch as inspired) were more influenced by him than any other book outside of our recognized canon. *The book of Enoch may inform and prepare us for coming events. Some believe there are prophecies in the Book of Enoch that are as applicable as those written in the books of Daniel and Revelation.*

So, take a comfortable seat alongside Holy Spirit and let Him bring you the download God wants you to receive from this ancestral blessing.

> *That you may hear from God's face*
> *what is told to you by Enoch* (2 En.36:1).

---

6   Lumpkin (cited above). Pages 10, 11, 16

Introduction

*M*y first taste of the Book of Enoch was suddenly interrupted - everything in me stood to alert and I began to tremble; God had showed up. (I still tear up recalling it.) I was reading how God commissioned Enoch to write all He had shown him, and gave him a deadline. Without words, I knew God was telling me to write about Enoch's assignment and make it accessible. Like many called by God before me, I had lots of 'Why me?'s – which He overrode as only God does. Neither was there room to niggle about the validity of Enoch's books; my call was to be obedient. God wanted these writings 'out there' - Now.

That personal epiphany was more than two years ago, 2019. I haven't met my deadline. But He assures me that, though late, it's not too late. Enoch posted vital information from God specifically to our time. He wants this special letter delivered and is using a fleet of couriers along the journey. He wants to infuse us with the faith and strength to negotiate the transition period we are now entering

> *through the 'culmination of all things'*
> *into God's glorious New Beginning.*

I am a missionary, 82 years old, not a scholar nor an academic. I do understand a little about culture and language and translation and editing, and about spirit kingdoms and realms. I too have a passion like Enoch had - to walk and talk with God and obey Him implicitly. He is my reason for living.

So, this book is not a theological study of the Book of Enoch. It doesn't include all his knowledge, or wisdom, or instructions. It's a layman's aid to understanding the letter your ancient ancestor sent you. Get and read it for yourself. It is your priceless ancestral blessing.

Of all the assignments God has given me over the years, (49 countries: remote unreached people groups; dark places, jealous for Jesus where He has never been named; strategic level war in spirit realms; altars of human sacrifice...) this assignment has been the hardest. Many times I cried, "Lord this is too hard, I can't do it." On the last occasion He replied:

> *"What I am commanding you today is not too difficult for you or beyond your reach. It is not up in heaven so that you have to ask, 'who will ascend into heaven and get it?' Nor is it beyond the sea so that you have to ask, 'who will cross the sea to get it and proclaim it to us so that we may obey it?' No, the word is very near you; it is in your mouth and in your heart so you may obey it"* (De.30:11-14).

I found Enoch difficult to understand. That's why I wanted to simplify him for ordinary folk - like me and my Pasifika and Asian families.

I have focussed on Enoch's text itself as my base, and have tried to keep free from the clamour of other voices and opinions. I wanted to listen to Enoch's voice. Enoch was writing before any of our Scriptures. If he is a true prophet of God his work will stand by itself. *Holy men of God spoke as they were moved by the Holy Spirit.* I needed Holy Spirit's help to see and understand things the way they were being revealed to Enoch. My preconceived ideas, and things I'd taken for granted, had to go. I have not tried to make a comprehensive list of links between Enoch and our Scriptures, but it will become obvious that his writings formed a large part of the data base of Biblical writers.

My editor-head so wanted to set Enoch all out in neat boxes to make sense of everything, but my linear, non-Hebrew mind had to be renewed. I've always been very geographically oriented; place and time were important to me. But I had to recognize that these are temporal things which will end. *For we look not at the things which are seen but at the things which are not seen, for the things which are seen are temporal, but the things that are not seen are eternal* (2Cor.4:18).

> God was taking Enoch outside of our
> finite time and geographic constraints
> and letting him live like the spirit-being
> Adam was created to be.

I was in unfamiliar territory and not at all sure, with all the intense study and analysis, that I was getting it right. That's when God said,

> *"Not only was the Teacher wise, but also he imparted knowledge to the people. He pondered and searched out and set in order many proverbs. The Teacher*

> *searched to find just the right words, and*
> **what he wrote was upright and true"**
> (Eccl.12:9,10).

That pretty closely described my labours, so the testimonial must also apply. That affirmation was a big hug!

I wrestled for some time to find the one **message** Enoch was sending. What is the one thing out of all this data he was wanting us to 'get'. One day the penny dropped. He had spelled it out in his very first line:

> *These are the words of Enoch's* **blessing**
> sent to his descendants living at the time when all
> unrighteousness is about to end.

God downloaded masses of data to Enoch which he obediently wrote down to pass on to us *so that you may know what is to come to pass*. This amazing data is scattered throughout the records of his visions and his celestial journeys. Sometimes the same journey may be retold, but recording different aspects. I have attempted to gather the data under what seem to be the main topics, again not comprehensive, but a general overview.

There are some standout things he surprisingly doesn't talk about. This work is about what Enoch has written, not what I expected or think he should say, nor have I tried to fit his material into my theologies. I have sought to be a strictly ethical editor and keep true to his voice. You and Holy Spirit will make the connections with words of later prophets familiar to us, and discern what God is saying to us specifically for our times.

Recently, thinking of the hurdles to publishing and distribution, God gave me this word from an underground House Church leader:

*"When the Lord reveals His will to us and we obey, our mission will be a **success regardless of the results**."*

You, reading these words, are part of that success! Bless you!

After many miles and millennia of miracles
Enoch's message has reached its destination.
To You with Love.
Enjoy!

Enoch's Books are Addressed to You
Yes, You!

*These are the words of Enoch's blessing in which he blessed **the righteous and the chosen ones**... not for my own generation, but for a generation far in the future (Enoch 1:1,2).[7]*

id you know you are a descendant of Enoch? Enoch was Noah's great-grandfather, so since we are all descended from Noah we are also descended from Enoch.

God let Enoch see all the way down the Telescope of Time to you at the other end of the Ages and told

---

7   All quotes are in italics, but quotes from Enoch are in blue to distinguish what he actually said.

him to pass on everything he knew to you *so you would know*.

So, Great-grandfather Enoch went to great lengths to send you this very special inheritance – his Blessing to you. He had a glimpse of his distant offspring faithfully walking in his footsteps at the other end of this long timeline – loving and serving the Ancient of Days; the God Enoch walked and talked with. He calls us 'The righteous' and the 'chosen ones'; in other places 'the holy ones', or 'the elect'. Those are comforting, embracing terms for us. You are a delight to the heart of God and to our ancient ancestor. He knew (in fact he prayed) that at the other end of life as we know it he would have descendants loving and following God.

About Enoch

What the Bible Says About Him

There aren't many mentions of Enoch in our scriptures, but they're pretty graphic.

- ***Enoch walked with God and God took him*** (Ge.5:24).

That's it! An extraordinary biography, brief and blunt.

It's like God is holding up a placard challenging us in these last days:

> "It's about to happen again.
> Walk with Me and I'll take you to be with Me."

- Hebrews displays the Honours Board for 'Heroes of Faith'. It puts Enoch right up there, saying:
  By faith Enoch was taken away so that he did not see death; …
  *He had this testimony, that **he pleased God*** (He.11:5).
  That was the reason!

- Jesus' brother, Jude, called him a Prophet and quoted his famous End-time prophecy:
  Now Enoch the seventh from Adam prophesied saying,

"See! The Lord is coming with thousands upon thousands of His holy ones to judge everyone, and to convict all the ungodly of all the corrupt things that were done in their depravity, and of all the harsh words that godless sinners have spoken against Him" (Jude 14,15) .[8]

---

8   En.1:9

Quotes. Other Biblical writers quote him, knowing that their readers for generations have learned Enoch's writings at their parents' knees.

- David's men quoted him: *"This is the day the Lord spoke of when He said to you [David] 'I will give your enemy into your hands for you to deal with as you wish'"* (1Sam.24:2,3).*9* **They were actually saying that Enoch's words were God's words.**

- And the prophet Micah - *The mountains will shake, and the high hills will be flattened, they will melt like wax before a flame, and the earth will be completely split apart, and everyone on earth will die and all mankind will be judged* (Mic.1:4).*10*

- Jesus quotes him: *It would have been better for them if they had never been born* (Mat.26:24, Mk.14:21).*11*

Enoch Echoes. They may not be direct quotes but they are repeating what Enoch has said. 'Enoch Echoes' are all through our scriptures: David's praise songs, Solomon's wisdom from science and nature, Job's understanding of creation, the visions of the

---

9   En.95:3
10   En.1:7
11   En.38:2

seers, Paul's talk about unrighteousness - all echo their ancestor. You will hear the echoes as you read Enoch. Our scripture writers were all so familiar with his writings that their language is sprinkled with his words and concepts.

The point is: If all these Holy men of God honour and use Enoch's texts, it is wisdom for us to pay attention to what he has written, especially since it was specifically addressed to us. I urge you to get your own copy of his letter to you.[12]

His Family Heritage

When Jude noted that Enoch was 'seventh from Adam' he placed him firmly in his hereditary setting and his historical time frame. That is: he was seven generations down from the first (and only) man God created. (See the chart.)

In fact, you'll notice that the first man, Great[6]Grandfather Adam, was still alive for most of Enoch's life. That meant that Enoch spent 308 growing-up years listening to G[6]G'dad Adam's stories.

Other Facts

Enoch was born about a millennium before the Great Flood (1034 years before), and he prophesied

12   See details in Fore Word.

its coming. He didn't get to meet his G'Grandson Noah, but sent a prophetic message to him by name. G'Grandad Enoch was caught up to Heaven (raptured) 59 years before Noah was born. And of course, Enoch clocked up a lot of 'first-mentions' in scripture – first scribe, writer, prophet, seer, preacher, astronomer, celestial traveller…

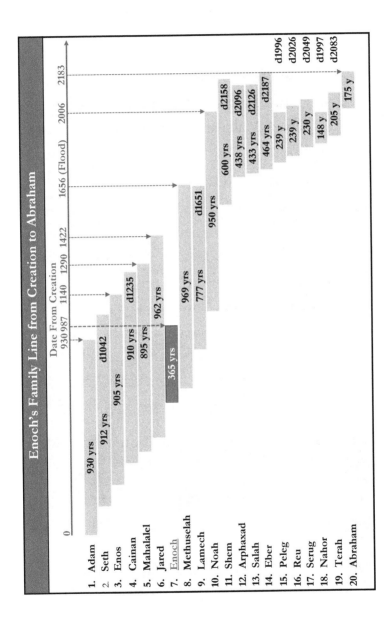

Enoch's Family Line from Creation to Abraham

Date From Creation

	0	930	987	1140	1290	1422	1656 (Flood)	2006	2183	
1. Adam		930 yrs								
2. Seth			912 yrs	d1042						
3. Enos			905 yrs							
4. Cainan				910 yrs	d1235					
5. Mahalalel				895 yrs						
6. Jared					962 yrs					
7. Enoch					365 yrs					
8. Methuselah						969 yrs				
9. Lamech						777 yrs	d1651			
10. Noah							950 yrs			
11. Shem								600 yrs	d2158	
12. Arphaxad								438 yrs	d2096	
13. Salah								433 yrs	d2126	
14. Eber								464 yrs	d2187	
15. Peleg								239 y		d1996
16. Reu								239 y		d2026
17. Serug								230 y		d2049
18. Nahor								148 y		d1997
19. Terah								205 y		d2083
20. Abraham								175 y		

What His Books Tells Us About Him

Young Enoch

Enoch was just learning to read when God gave him his first vision. Later, while still a youth living in his grandfather Mahalalel's[13] house, he saw another 'terrible' vision.

Heaven collapsed and was torn down and fell to the earth. And when it fell to earth, I saw how the earth was swallowed up in a great abyss, and mountains were suspended on mountains, and hills sank down on hills, and high trees were ripped from their stems, and hurled down and sunk in the abyss. I lifted up my voice to cry aloud, and said: "The earth is destroyed!" And my grandfather Mahalalel woke me as I lay near him, and said to me: Why do you cry so my son, and why do you make such moaning?"

His grandfather interprets the vision and gives him advice.

I recounted to him the whole vision which I had seen, and he said to me:
"You have seen a terrible thing, my son. Your dream is of a grave time and concerns the secrets of all the sin of the earth: it must sink into the abyss and be

13   Mahalal = praise, El = God

totally destroyed. And now, my son, arise and pray to the Lord of Glory since you are a believer, that a remnant may remain on the earth, and that He may not destroy the whole earth. My son, from heaven all this will come on the earth, and on the earth there will be great destruction."

Enoch's Obedience

After that I arose and prayed and implored God and wrote down my prayer for the generations of the world (En.83:2-10).

I find Enoch's record of this event quite amusing: On going outside he was most relieved to find the sky still there - a few stars still out, the moon setting, and the sun rising in the east – everything was still normal! He was human too.

Enoch's Worship

He lifted up his hands and spoke with 'the tongue God gave all flesh to bless Him with':

"Blessings to you, O Lord, King, Great and mighty in your greatness, Lord of the whole creation of heaven, King of kings and God of the whole world. Your power and kingship and greatness abide forever and ever, and throughout all generations your dominion, and all heavens are your throne forever, and the whole earth

your footstool forever and ever. For you have made and rule all things, and nothing is too hard for you, wisdom never departs from the place of your throne. You know and see and hear everything, and there is nothing hidden from you for you see everything (En.84:2,3).

Enoch's Discernment and Intercession

He continues his prayer: *"And now the angels of your heavens are guilty of trespass, and on the flesh of men abides your wrath until the great day of judgment... And now my Lord, destroy from the earth the flesh which has aroused your wrath, but the flesh of righteousness and uprightness establish as an eternal plant bearing seed forever, and hide not your face from the prayer of your servant, O Lord"* (En.84:4).

Enoch's passion

From his earliest days Enoch had a passion for God – a passion to develop the kind of relationship with God that his G[6] Grandfather Adam had experienced.

As a child Enoch heard first-hand from G[6]G'dad Adam:

- About the glory before the Cosmic Disaster we call The Fall

- what it was like walking and talking with the Creator of the universes

- what the Beginning was like and the original Garden
- how God meant everything to operate (Maker's instructions)
- how man and God and nature co - operated together in harmony.

These conversations shaped his life with the passion that saw him eventually walking as a companion of God, like early Adam.

"I longed to live there, and my spirit longed for that habitation: and so it became my portion" (En.39:8).

Enoch's passion pleased God Who responded, even in his early years, by visiting him with dreams and visions. He showed Enoch secrets past and mysteries of things not yet come. [Later another prophet explains that *God does nothing before revealing His secrets to His servants the prophets* (Amos 3:7).]

Don't be surprised to see this happening again – children and youth being given powerful visions, insights and words from God in these end times. Nurture their hunger and receptivity for God. The value of a godly heritage is beyond calculation.

Enoch's Righteousness

The introduction to Book 1, says: "*Enoch was a righteous man, whose eyes were opened by God so that he saw a vision of the Holy One in the heavens* (En.1:2).

God testified of his righteousness when Enoch was fearful at being ushered into God's presence, *bowing his face to the ground. "Fear not Enoch, you are a righteous man."*

He was a righteous man living in a fast-degenerating society – a society which was hurtling towards the Flood.

Enoch's Extra-terrestrial Travels

God responded to Enoch's passion to know and walk with Him by taking him out of earth's realms into the heavens. God unlocked physical boundaries for Enoch and allowed him to access realms normally only spirit beings could enter. He showed him the mysteries of creation, the origins of stars and wind and lightnings and the wonders of how the universe worked. He got to see God's Throne and His awesome holiness. God and Enoch talked and travelled together, God sharing His secrets with His friend.

God so enjoyed Enoch's company (after all that's why He created man) that on one visit He just let him stay on – move in and stay permanently with Him!

Is it any wonder that in this last decade interest has been growing in Enoch and his books?

I believe, in these last days, as we approach the end of this era, there will be more Enochs – more comings and goings between God's other realms.

It's already happening. After all we are spirit-beings, temporarily housed in these tent-bodies. Shortly they will be exchanged for a glorious body fit for our new multi-realm roles.

Invisible Realms

He Who is invisible, and lives in the invisible realm, promises to show Himself to us! *He who has my commandments and keeps them, he it is who loves Me; and I will love him and will* **manifest Myself to Him** (Jn.14:21). This is my favourite verse; I tear up thinking about how He has done that for me - in precious unexpected and intimate ways. The privilege of it!

The thinning veil. The veil is getting thinner – it has been for a while now. The separation between the natural and spiritual realms is growing less defined. We see more passing through from this world to the other and experience more visitations from the other realm - more comings and goings both ways – more angel visitations and more visits to heaven. There's coming a merging, a less inhibited communicating across the line.

We are awakening to the truth that we are **spirit beings** –temporarily housed in a 'temporal' body. We are gradually beginning to accept the possibilities of this and at the doorway shiver at the limitless expanse of those possibilities!

As usual, the secular world caught on quicker than we did. We are supposed to be the custodians of God's spiritual laws, and the understanding of spirit realms. In the dark kingdom they have been travelling and communicating and understanding spiritual realms and possibilities that, for a long time, the church has denied exist. Now the media has caught on and is proliferating possibilities visually before our eyes, conditioning spiritually deprived, hungry generations to accept and engage with multiple dimensions.

Only God knows how many realms there are out there, but one thing He made clear: He separated the Light from the Darkness. There is a realm of darkness; it is ruled by the prince of the powers of darkness and death, and the powers of the air. The Kingdom of Light is ruled by the Lord of Light and Life. God set a door to the authentic Kingdom of

Light; it is His Son, Jesus the Christ. No one enters this kingdom except through Him. If you have accessed a spirit realm through some other way you are in the kingdom of darkness. Beat a retreat and find the right Door!

Why Enoch?

God is looking for people with a passion like Enoch's – people who just want to enjoy His company. Is that you? The Father's heart longs for an intimate relationship with His children. He's listening for that echo responding from earth. We are entering a time like Enoch's when knowing the Creator is essential.

God is about to take His creation back. His plan is to restore it to how He made it before the Fall, when:
everything He saw was "good"!

Can you imagine what it was like?
A sea of Love and mutual enjoyment.
No negatives or opposites or opposition
or opponents,
no contra, controversy or counter, no anti only unity,
no wrong only right, nothing false only truth,
no darkness no shadow just Light,
no enemies only loved ones,

no tension or stress just rest,
nothing to fear or be wary of;
absolute trust and harmony,
no evil, just good everywhere.

Only one "Don't" – **one** forbidden fruit!

He is about to restore that paradise, and to do that He has to destroy all evil from the face of the earth. That's why He wants you to get this information from your ancestor Enoch, who saw the whole history of earth unfolding before his eyes. The Timeless One, the Creator, is taking back what is His. Enoch saw the End and the glorious Afterwards.

Enoch's Task

God told Enoch to *declare everything to your son Methuselah to preserve it and to deliver the words to the generations of the world. Write all My words in their languages and do not change or minish.*

Tell your sons all that I have told you, and all that you have seen, from the lower heaven up to my throne, and all the troops. Give them the books of the handwriting, and they will read them and will know Me for the creator of all things, and will understand how there is **no other God but Me** (En.33:7-9).

Riddle:

Methuselah, Enoch's son, was

'the oldest man who ever lived

who died before his father did'.

Answer:

Methuselah died at 969 years old (see

the chart), but his father, Enoch, never

died! God just took him off the

planet.

So Enoch wrote books recording all He was shown. Included are graphic descriptions of unknown things similar those depicted by prophets like Daniel, Ezekiel and John. He included a warning and instructions to his great-grandson, Noah, about the Flood. Then he passed on all the precious manuscripts to Methuselah his son with instructions to care for and pass them on, not just to Noah, but from generation to generation to **the last generation** at the end of time - when all the things Enoch saw would climax.

Take these books of your father's handwriting and read them. For the books are many,[14] *and in them you will*

---

14   Three Books of Enoch have been found, not all complete. One has an insertion from the Book of Noah.

learn all the Lord's works, all that has been from the beginning of creation, and will be till the end of time. And if you will observe my hand-writing, you will not sin against the Lord, because there is no other except the Lord, neither in heaven, nor in earth, nor in the very lowest places, nor in the one foundation (2 En.47:2-4).

Methuselah's task was not an easy one, especially with the destruction of the Great Flood pending. There were only two methods to pass on the information:

written - physically preserving and passing on his 'books'

spoken - orally sharing his message and knowledge from parents to children every generation forever, so that everyone knew.

Today communication technology has exploded, so that even printers, presses, recorders, film, are becoming obsolete and replaced with ever newer methods. Then, with only hand writing and carving, oral traditions were very important, as they still are today in some tribal cultures – the stories of the elders passed down word-of-mouth to the grandchildren.

Methuselah, whose name means 'his death will initiate', lived until the very year his grandson, Noah, completed building the Ark - the escape vessel God had ordered. Methuselah's extra-long life stands as a signpost to God's mercy - patiently waiting. He provided an escape. Makes me think of the inspiring hope of the old negro-spiritual: *'Git on board li'l chillen, git on board'*.

Peter describes that time like this: *Even though God waited patiently all the days that Noah built his ship, only a few were saved then, eight to be exact* (1Pe.3:19 Msg).

Which is precisely why I want to get this information to you - to make sure a great many more than eight will take heed and be saved at the end of this era.

Get in the Ark. The Ark is God !

Grandad Methuselah personally passed on Enoch's warning of the coming disaster to Noah and his sons, and maybe even assisted Noah building the Ark. Certainly it was Methuselah's responsibility to make sure the precious writings of his prophet father, Enoch, were carefully stored away on the Ark and preserved from the destruction of the deluge.

Enoch Now

Right now, Enoch is with an ever-growing 'cloud of witnesses' hanging over the balconies of Heaven cheering us on. Some have been there thousands of years waiting for us to come and to roll up the scroll of history so that together we can move into the final chapter and possess the new heavens and new earth that God has prepared for those who love Him.

Those departed saints on the balcony (sometimes called 'men in white linen' or 'souls of just men made perfect') have also looked through the telescope of the Ancient of Days. While here on earth *they had their eyes on the One no eyes can see, and kept right on going. They saw way off a far better country – heaven country* (Heb.11:16). Hebrews 11 is the chapter about the great heroes of faith, their tenacious focus and their mighty deeds, '*some who under torture, refused to give up and go free, preferring something better*' (v.37). They **saw the invisible** realm and unswervingly set their faces towards it. (*For we look not at the things which are seen, but at the things which are not seen; for the things which are seen are temporal, but the things that are not seen are eternal* (2Cor:4:18).)

But the Faith Chapter goes on to record that not one of those hero patriarchs received what they were believing God for! I was shocked to read this. Then I wept at what follows:

Because **without us** *they are not complete!*

They are waiting for us,

the Last Days generation that closes the chapter on this earth's history. *Only together with us would they be made perfect (NIV). God had a better plan for us: that their faith and our faith would come together to make one completed whole* (Heb.11:40Msg).

Like Enoch they saw the invisible and they are waiting for us to complete God's plan and become one with them. This is 'the Completion', the 'Culmination of the Ages', for which all heaven is hanging out. *The day of consummation, the great judgment in which the age will be consummated, over the Watchers and the godless* (En.16:1). They want to wind this era up, so we can move on into the Promise.

Hebrews 12 (Msg) goes on to say, *Do you see what this means? These veterans cheering us on? It means we'd better get on with it. Strip down and start running – and never quit! No extra spiritual fat, no parasitic sins.*

Keep your eyes on Jesus. *He both began and finished this race we're in.*
He never lost sight of where He was headed – He could put up with anything along the way: Cross, shame, whatever. And now He's there for the joy set before Him (Heb.12 :1-3).

The Days of Enoch

Enoch knew what troubled times were like. It was during his father Jared's time that the Fallen Angels unleashed their evil on earth. He experienced earth plunging headlong into the 'Days of Noah', with the build-up of evil so intense that God decided to destroy the whole thing. Through it all Enoch pulled in ever closer to God and God showed him what He was going to do about it.

This is what God is looking for right now, those who love Him drawing in close to Him as troubles increase.

God's mercy found a man 'perfect in his generations'[15], Enoch's G'Grandson, Noah. He planned to save Noah and his family from the global destruction and to start a new earth.

After Noah's time and its turmoil, Enoch saw through to the increase of evil in our times. And he saw God again pull the curtain on earth like He did then. *As it was in the Days of Noah so shall it be in the day when the Son of Man is revealed* (Lk.17:26,30). That's a very encouraging verse for us. That's when the Son of Man will be revealed, which is what we're longing for. After all, He is our long-awaited Bridegroom.

Peter saw that time too. *The heavens will disappear with a roar; the elements will be destroyed by fire, and the earth and everything in it will be laid bare. Since*

---

15   Expanded in chapter 3.

*everything will be destroyed in this way, what kind of people ought you to be? You ought to live holy and godly lives as you **look forward to** the day of God and speed its coming. In keeping with his promise, we are looking forward to a new heaven and a new earth, the home of righteousness* (2Pe.3).

Enoch could see the New Earth and the New Heavens - after God destroyed all evil. … *Then I will cause my Chosen One to dwell with them [those who have called upon My glorious name], and I will transform the heaven and make it an eternal blessing and light and I will transform the earth and make it a blessing and let my chosen ones live there; but the sinners and evildoers shall not set foot on it. My righteous ones are satisfied and at peace because I have caused them to live in My Presence* (En.45:4-6).

So Enoch is sending us, his descendants, this blessing as an encouragement to stay focussed and see these times through to the end. He keeps trying to describe the glory that awaits. It's obviously so far beyond anything we know that, no matter how painful things may become, it's worth it.

Hang in there, we have:

- his ancestral blessing

- this understanding of the past, and knowledge of the future
- the host of witnesses enthusiastically cheering us on
- God's unbreakable promises – signed with His Son's blood
- a future worth dying for.

I am deeply moved at the privilege of being chosen to see this last generation. You were specifically chosen for such a time as this. The focus of all heaven and all of history climaxes with the times we are entering! Prophets and men and angels have looked forward with awe to this time. We have their attention!

Hold tight, all things are about to change.

The King is coming

About his Books

Mark well the words of your father, which are all come to you ***from YHWH's lips*** (2 En.47:1).
And wise men will seek the truth and they and their sons will understand the words of this book, and recognize that their riches shall not be able to save them or overcome their sins (En.100:6).

To hold in our hands books written so long ago is awesome. Yet apparently Enoch's books are not the first books written by man. Although Enoch was writing before the Great Flood[16], he actually

---

16   1656AA, the year of Methuselah's death. James Ussher, *The Annals of the World.* See also chart, Ch.1.

mentions books written by his forefathers, including Adam (2 En.47:6).

The Theme

God is about to take His creation back.

This is the best of news, but Enoch wants to make sure you're on the same page with Him. The destruction of everything not in His plan is imminent – rebellion, God-rejection, evil will be finished.

The intricacies of creation, he explains, show God's glory and His desire to reveal Himself to mankind. Since everything in God's creation follows the exact pattern set for it, how important it is for us to do so.

The Beginning. He tells how fallen angels corrupted creation and evil exploded, and he details their judgment and the destruction of sin.

Before the End. A huge cleansing is coming. He is restoring everything to original condition, gutting the building. He describes life just before the end - what it will be like in the end times – and sends blessing and promises for those in the last generation. They will be safe and need not fear.

After the End. He gives us pictures of life after the end of all evil, when God restores everything back to His original plan. It's hard to explain the Majesty and Glory of operations under Divine rule.

Hidden Mysteries. Enoch's books contain hidden mysteries regarding:

- Other realms – light and dark, doors, hell, abodes of the dead
- Creation, and workings of the universe
- The secret name that holds everything together
- Eternity

World History

Enoch wrote the complete history of Earth - not in retrospect as historians do, but as a prophet or seer does - as a spectator watching the future rolling out before him. [Like John's Revelation of things past, present and to come (Rev 1:19).] He wrote two versions, in two parables: The Parable of Weeks (En.93:1-10; 91:12-17 in this order), and The Animal Apocalypse (En.85-90); they are parallel accounts.

The Parable of Weeks describes 10 weeks, not necessarily of any specific time length, but indicating periods or eras.

In the 7th week the 'Great Apostacy' arises, *when sin and unrighteousness and* *blasphemy and violence in all kinds of deeds increase, and apostasy and transgression and uncleanness increase, a great chastisement shall come from heaven upon all these, and the holy Lord will come forth with wrath and chastisement to execute judgment on earth.*

Apostacy is a rejection of God's laws. We see many examples of this happening in both society and church today. People think, "The laws do not apply to us today, nor the miracles, nor gifts, nor spiritual power, nor apostles and prophets". Increasing numbers of churches accept abortion, divorce, sex outside marriage, homosexual marriage, homosexual priests, and many other practices abhorrent to God. Apostacy is a deliberate reversal of the covenant with a holy God.

In the 8th week, the 'week of righteousness', *a sword shall be given by which righteous judgment may be executed on the oppressors and they be delivered into the hands of the righteous.* The Sword of the Spirit has been given to believers to combat and defeat evil spiritual powers. This passage describes an era when the saints rise up in powerful spiritual warfare. It is in this week *a house shall be built for the kingly Temple of the Great One in His glorious splendour, for all generations forever* (En.91:12). This may not be a physical house, but refer to the spiritual temple built without hands of which we are the 'lively stones'.

In the 9th week *the righteous judgment shall be revealed...and all the workers of wickedness shall completely pass from the earth, and they will be cast into the pit. The world will be written down for destruction. And all mankind* [remaining] *shall look to the path of uprightness* [follow righteousness].

And after this, *at the end of the 10th week, there shall be the great eternal judgment, in which He will execute judgment among the angels. And the first heaven shall depart and pass away, and a new heaven shall appear, and all the powers of the heavens shall give sevenfold light. And after that there will be many weeks **without number for ever**, and all shall be in goodness and righteousness, and sin shall no more be mentioned for ever* (En.91:14-17).

So, in the 9th week there is a judgment, and all unrighteousness and evil 'pass from the earth'. Then at the **end** of the 10th week[17] there is another judgment – of the angels particularly - at which juncture the counting of time ceases and 'weeks without number forever' follow. Eternity begins.

The Animal Parable repeats the story of the Parable of Weeks but focuses on the Lord's sheep, the righteous.

A Sword for the Sheep. *And I saw till a great sword was given to the sheep, and the sheep proceeded against all the beasts of the field to slay them* [previously beasts were tearing and devouring the sheep], *and all the beasts and the birds of the heaven fled before their face.* When the saints took their sword to the enemy, he fled.

The Lord Finishes the Battle. *And I saw the Lord of the sheep came to them with His staff of wrath and He smote the earth. The earth split open, and all the beasts and all*

---

17   This period seems to refer to 'the Millennium' though is not given this time frame. The 10th Week follows the destruction of evil and establishing of righteousness. Judgments book-end this week, both ushering it in and closing it out.

the birds of the heaven fell from among those sheep, and were swallowed up in the earth and it covered them. When the saints rose up to war the Lord joined them with great destruction, assisted by the earth.[18]

The Lord comes to judge. The Lord of the sheep then came, erected His throne and sat there while books were opened before Him. First to be judged was the star[19] which led other stars astray. They were all judged guilty *and were cast into an abyss, full of fire and flaming, and full of pillars of fire.* Abusive shepherds and blind sheep were also judged and sent there.

The Lord replaces His House. Enoch watched the old house folded up and carried away with all its ornaments. *I stood up to see till the Lord of the sheep brought a new house, greater and loftier than the first, and set it up in the place of the first which had been folded up: all its pillars were new, and its ornaments were new and larger than*

18   See Nu. 16 for a biblical story of earth swallowing the rebellious.
19   Lucifer the initial rebel leader, including the angels involved in the genetic pollution of mankind. (See Ch.4)

those of the old one which He had taken away, and all the sheep were in it.

The Sword returned. *And I saw them lay down that sword which had been given to the sheep, and they brought it back into the house, and it was sealed before the presence of the Lord. And those sheep were all white, and their wool was abundant and clean.* All the beasts and birds obeyed the sheep in everything. (Restoration of Adam's mandate to have dominion on the earth.)

All Return. *And all that had been dispersed, and all the beasts of the field, and all the birds of the heaven, assembled in that house, and the Lord of the sheep rejoiced with great joy because they were all good[20] and had returned to His house* (En.90:19-34).

'All Good'. This is God's dream fulfilled: a faithful creation all at peace, together in His house, swords put away for good.

Publication

Enoch was commanded to write, and the content was given by God – Who told him who to address it

---

20   'Good' as He had pronounced at creation.

to, because: **what was about to hit Noah's day was going to hit ours**.

God gave him one year to record and teach all the things He had shown him, and *give his last commands* to his children. In the following year he would be taken from them (En.81:6).

Apply your mind, Enoch, and know Him Who is speaking to you, and take the books you have written and go down to earth and let them distribute the books of your handwriting — children to children, generation to generation, nations to nations (2 En. 47:6).

- *that all may hear from My face what is told them by you* (So Enoch became an interface between the people and God – as we containers of God may also.)
- *that they may read and understand, how there is no other God but me.*
- *And that they may always keep my commandments*
- *and begin to read and take in the books of your handwriting* (En.36: 1,2).

Enoch gathered his descendants and said: *The Spirit is poured out upon me[21], that I may show you everything that shall befall you forever* (En.91:1),

---

21 Compare scripture writers moved by the Holy Ghost 2 Pe.1:21.

And now my son Methuselah, all these things I am recounting to you and writing down for you. I have revealed to you everything and given you books concerning all these: so preserve, my son, the books from your father's hand and see that you deliver them to the generations of the world (En.82:1).

Food Distribution down the millennia! Enoch intentionally sent imperishable spiritual food and sustenance down the millennia to us!

It shall please those that eat thereof better than good food (En.82:3).

Distribute into all your generations, and amongst the nations who shall have the sense to fear God, let them receive the books, and may they come to love them more than any food or earthly sweets, and read them and apply themselves to them (En.48:5,6).

Compare:

- the Word of God being our food (Jn 6:51)
- Jesus being the Bread of Life (Jn.6:35)
- and sweeter than honey (Ps.119:103)
- and Paul's talk about spiritual meat for the mature (Heb 5:13,14).

In fact, Enoch notes that even inanimates *believe and glorify YHWH with all their power and that their food is in every act of thanksgiving. They thank and glorify and extol the name of YHWH forever and ever* (En.69:24).

Future Hunger, Future Glory

God tells Enoch: *From your seed* (Flood survivors) *shall arise another generation, much afterwards[22], but of them many will be very insatiate. He who raises that generation, shall reveal to them the books of your handwriting, and of your fathers, to them to whom he must point out the guardianship of the world[23], to the faithful men and workers of My pleasure, who do not acknowledge My name in vain. And they shall tell another generation, and **those others having read shall be glorified thereafter, more than the first** (2 En.35:1-3).

I find this an exciting prophecy – an encouragement to Enoch about the destiny of his books, and also to us who approach the last generation and are reading his words. So the last generation will have an insatiable hunger for spiritual things, and their mentors/elders will reveal the Books of Enoch (and his forebears?[24]) to these last days believers, and the glory of the

---

22 Recent translation: the last of many (generations)
23 Recent translation: the earthly guardians of the books will show them to men of faith.
    Andrei A. Orlov, The Heirs of the Enochic Lore: "Men of Faith" in 2 Enoch 35:2 and Sefer Hekhalot 48D:10. https://www.marquette.edu/maqom/vera.html
24 We may even yet see legitimate copies of Adam, Seth, Enos, Cainan, Mahalalel, or Jared's books!

Lord will fall on them 'more than in the beginning'. Think of the glory on Adam in the Garden - more than that. Or is it the Light intensifying on God's people in the end, or is it our glorified bodies passing into the new Heavens? But it does mean that as we approach these times, the books of Enoch play a role in the Glory of the Lord increasing to a level never before experienced. That is some awesome power! And I hope you noted that wonderful blessing to God's faithful workers who 'do not labour in vain'.

Précis - Enoch Summarizes his Writings

He writes very directly – a no-nonsense style telling things exactly as he saw them. He laid out a nutshell version of his writings in his first chapter.

Chapter 1- a general summary or overview of what he's written.

Introduction of himself: [author blurb]

> *Enoch was a righteous man, his eyes were opened by God and he saw this vision of the Holy One in the heavens* (which Angels explained to him).

Who he's writing to [target audience]:

> *not for my own generation, but for a generation far in the future* (En.1:2).

> The implication is, God is looking for righteous men like Enoch with a passion to

walk with Him. He wants to open their eyes to see heavenly things, and prepare them for what is to come.

What he's writing [content]:

These are the words of Enoch's Blessing

Why he's writing [purpose]:

In which he blessed the righteous and the chosen ones

Where the audience will be [location]:

Who will live in the time of the tribulation

Woops! That's not what we expected. Weren't we taught that we (the righteous!) would get raptured away and not see the 'tribulation'? But Enoch is saying the righteous will be here.

When [time frame]:

When all the wicked and those who have rejected God will be removed (En.1:1)

Here He defines the 'Tribulation' for us: the time when God removes all the wicked and God-rejecters.

So, it's Enoch's blessing to the righteous

who live while the wicked (= those who have rejected God) are being removed (called the tribulation).

He goes on to *'prophesy'* (Verses 2-7) about

The Great and Holy One:

He will come and walk on Earth showing His awesome strength.

Everyone will be terrified, especially the Watchers (Fallen Angels).

Earth shakes, hills melt, and the earth completely splits apart!

And everyone on the earth will die and all mankind will be judged (v.7).

BUT – [here come the Blessings]: (v.8)[25]

1. *But He will establish peace through the righteous.*

2. *He will protect His chosen ones and put them under His mercy.*

3. *They will all belong to God and they will prosper,*

4. *and He will bless them.*

5. *He will help every one of them,*

6. *and light will come to them,*

7. *and He will establish peace through them.*
   (repeat of #1)

---

25   This is exactly how the verse reads. I have inserted the bullet points to emphasize the points he is making.

Enoch ends his summary (v.9) with his apocalyptic (end-time) prophecy which Jude quotes word for word in our Bible (Jd.14,15).

- *See! The Lord is coming*
- *with thousands upon thousands of His holy ones*
- *to judge everyone,*
- *and to convict all the ungodly of all the corrupt things that were done in their depravity,*
- *and of all the harsh words that godless sinners have spoken against Him.*

Here's the good news (v.9):

A righteous Judge is coming. What for?

> To whisk away the righteous and chosen, and rescue them from the conquering evil? A resounding, NO!
>
> He is coming victorious, as sovereign Lord, to judge and convict the wicked, to deal with corruption and abuse.
>
> He is coming to liberate, bring peace and restore creation back to His original dream.

The Climax: See! The Lord is Coming

This is the major and most awesome event Enoch sees down that telescope of the ages. He's posting the spiritual picture over the airwaves to us. It's prime news. He's trying to hand us the telescope. He wants us to **see,** like he does. He describes with word pictures, but this one thing he actually tells us to see – *"See! The Lord is coming. Thousands upon thousands and tens of thousands of His saints are coming with Him."* "Open your spirit eyes and see this (or use the holy imagination God gave you). The End is in sight. Don't give up now. See, the Holy Ones from the balconies of Heaven are on their way with Him. Shortly you'll all be together bringing the climax of the Age." Isaiah repeats this 'see' theme: *"Behold (see) your God! Behold He comes with a strong hand and His arm shall rule for him, behold His reward is with Him"* (Is.40:10).

Who is this that's coming?

Who is this, causing such excitement? David famously asks a similar question:

Who is this King of Glory?
The Lord strong and mighty,
the Lord mighty in battle.
Lift up your heads oh you gates and
the King of glory shall come in.
The Lord of hosts,
He is the King of glory

(Ps.24:7-10).

In all his walking with God and his visits to other realms, what impacted Enoch most was visiting God Enthroned.

Throne Room Encounters

The house was built of flames of fire. It so excelled in splendour that I cannot describe it to you. I saw a **lofty throne**; *its appearance was like crystal and its wheels like a sun, and there were cherubim. And from underneath the throne came streams of flaming fire so that I could not look at it. And* **the Great Glory** *sat on it…. no flesh could behold Him. 10,000 x 10,000 stood before Him …*

Enoch's Reaction: *I had been prostrate on my face, trembling; and the Lord, YHWH, called me with His Own mouth and said to me, "Come here Enoch and hear My Word." One of the Holy Ones waked me, and made me rise up and approach the door, and I bowed my face. And He* ['the Great Glory'!] *said to me, and I heard His voice: "Do not be afraid Enoch, you righteous man and scribe of righteousness: approach and hear My voice"* (En.14:16-15:1).

Noah had a similar experience (recorded in the fragment of Noah's writings inserted into Enoch's book). He saw a great quaking that made even the heavens shake. He saw, the Most High on His Throne, the angels, and 1000,000s and 10,000 x 10,000. *And* *a great trembling seized me, and fear took hold of me, and my legs gave way, and I melted with weakness and I fell upon my face.* Michael sent an angel to pick him up 'and his spirit returned' (En.60:1-6).

On one 'Crystal Palace' visit (En.71:5-17) Enoch collapses again and cries out with a loud voice and 'with the spirit of power' and 'blesses' and 'glorifies' and 'exalts' the Most Holy One. This worship pleases the Lord and an angel comes to Enoch introducing the Enthroned One.

> *"**This is the Son of Man** who is **born** to righteousness…He proclaims to you Shalom in the name of the world to come, for from Him has proceeded shalom since the creation of the world."*

Enoch describes how he saw with his own eyes the **Chosen One of righteousness** (Son of Man) and saw His habitation (En.39:6). *And my face was changed because I could not take in any more* (En.39:14). [Remember Moses' face after seeing God on Sinai? That event too was a new revelation to Moses of Who God was – I AM.]

A new revelation of Who God is

This introduction to the Son of Man was a new revelation of God to Enoch.

He consequently often uses the title, **Son of Man.**[26]

Other titles[27] and descriptions he uses as his revelation expands are:

'Fountain of Righteousness',

'Light of the gentiles',

'Hope of the troubled',

'Life-giver', 'Protector',

'Staff to the righteous'

   - who will lean on Him to brace themselves and not fall.

Inexhaustible 'Spring of wisdom'

   - from whom thirsty souls drink and as a result are filled with wisdom and live with the righteous, holy and elect.

Significant things to notice about Enoch's remarkable revelation in this 'crystal palace' encounter, above (Chapter 71):

1. The Son of Man was not yet revealed at the time. Remember this is pre Flood, pre Abraham, pre Moses. Yet Enoch prophesies:

---

26 See examples and descriptions in En.46:1-4; 48:2-10, and regarding His role as Judge: En.69:27,29, etc.

27 See particularly chapters 48 and 49.

the Son of Man was born,

was present at the creation of the world,

And He carried all the above titles -

all while He was still 'the mystery' not yet revealed (Col. 1:26).

2. Our worship is pleasing to God

and results in further revelation of Who He is (En.71:14).

3. Our thirsting to drink from His springs not only fills us with wisdom,

but links us to the realm of the holy and elect

where we can live by the Spirit (En.48:1).

Interfacing Flesh with the Lord of Spirits. Enoch's and Noah's physical bodies reacted at some of their encounters with the Lord of spirits – collapsing, trembling, even shouting in the Presence of the Holy One. Angels sometimes have to stand Enoch on his feet for His audience with God. So, this is not just a Pentecostal phenomenon post 1906. Many have experienced being overwhelmed / 'wasted' in His Presence. It gives credibility to phenomena we may have questioned, scorned, or been embarrassed about. We've mostly missed (or dismissed) such accounts in scripture.[28]

So, Enoch has a deep and holy awe of the Creator God Who has invited him (and us) into this amazing friend relationship. One of the initial points God wanted Enoch to make to his family was:

> *Show to all your children that no flesh is righteous in the sight of the Lord for He is their Creator* (En.81:5).

This is a necessary understanding before *the Holy Great One, the Lord of Glory, the Eternal King, comes down to sit on His throne and inhabit the earth with goodness* (En.25:3). Our flesh is stripped of its own power in His Presence, and we are made very aware it is only by His strength we live and function.

All this becomes starkly relevant when Enoch is talking about the good news that this God is coming with multiple tens of thousands of His holy ones. If a righteous man like Enoch can't handle the Presence of the Holy One and His hosts, can you imagine the reaction of God-rejecters and God-haters? *Unrighteousness will not be able to save itself: at His judgment the unrepentant will crumble before Him* (En.50:4).

---

28   Saul on the way to Damascus. King Saul humiliated before God's prophets, 1Sam.19:24. The priests unable to stand when God's glory showed up in the temple, 2Chron.5:14, are other examples of people physically overcome by the presence of God.

However, be encouraged, not all God-encounters are debilitating. Moses was able to approach God in the quaking and fire on the mountain, when the people were saying "you go for us, we can't face Him". And later the 70 elders went up the mountain into His presence - and ate with Him!

"Fear not Enoch," God said to him, *"You are a righteous man"* (En.15:1). Enoch keeps telling his descendants not to fear.

So what does it all mean for us in our circumstances?

1. Get used to increasing encounters with God and His holiness and His cleansing.
2. God wants to walk with us into more dimensions and understandings as His new era approaches.
3. Be willing to go with Him into unfamiliar places.
4. Practise knowing His voice and doing whatever He tells you to do.
5. Get ready to be living with Him permanently. He is moving in.

Vision of Jesus Waiting

We are living in the time of this vision. Are we some of those blind to the revelation of His Presence and His imminent intent? God wants His people ready – for anything.

I saw Jesus standing at the front of our congregation with His back towards us. He was holding His hand out to the side like a parent waiting for a child to take His hand and go. But the people were busy, unaware He was there – unaware of His Presence. They were busy packing and chatting and loading their donkeys with all they would take on their journey with Jesus. The only ones aware of Him were some little children sitting at His feet in physical contact with Him – sitting very still, acutely aware He was waiting to go, standing there in His everyday robe and sandals.

I wanted to take His hand saying, "I'm ready Jesus". But the vision was a still and I didn't know whether we would set off, or if He would keep waiting for the oblivious people. And, if we left, would some suddenly realize and run to catch up? I only knew we were to go on a journey with Jesus, but no one was aware He was about to leave.

We had never been on this road before, a road where we needed our hand in His - to both show us the way and to steady us in the rough places.

Everyone knew about the journey, but even in church many were about to miss it. Their focus was on things and fellowship and preparation – anything but Jesus Himself. Only the children with their sensitive spirits sensed His loneliness and desire to leave. They were ready to go.

Expect Signs

- **Revelations of the Son of Man.** Peter says Jesus *was foreordained before the foundation of the world, but was* **manifest in these last times for you** (1Pe.1:20). Jesus is the 'mystery' of God being unveiled more fully in these times. *From the beginning, the Son of Man was hidden and the Most High preserved Him and revealed Him to the chosen* (En.62:7).

  - Increasing revelations of the Son of God and the Messiah's Name.

  - "Aha!" moments – sudden divine enlightenments – God showing up.

- Increasing exposure of evil and lies, along with both conviction of sin and lightbulb moments where people recognize the Truth.

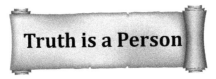

Truth is a Person

- God, revealing mysteries He told the prophets to seal up and hide until now (John, Daniel, Ezekiel). This book itself is a sign – Enoch's writings hidden for so long, reaching their destination.[29]

- *Books will be given to the righteous and the wise to become a cause of joy and uprightness and much wisdom…and they shall believe in them and rejoice over them* (En.104:12).

- A rush of prophecies being fulfilled. A 'sign' is a 'sign'-ificant event on God's calendar. Here I believe is one such **sign**ificant event – a sign and a prophecy fulfilled.

Five millennia ago the prophet Enoch, *saw another host of wagons, and men riding thereon, and coming on the winds from the east, and from the west and the south. And the noise of their wagons was heard, and*

---

29   See Fore Word

when this turmoil took place the holy ones from heaven remarked it, and the pillars of the earth were moved from their place, and the sound thereof was heard from the one end of heaven to the other, in one day. And they shall all fall down and worship the Lord of Spirits (En.57:1-3).

A Prophetic Sign

In 2017 a host of peoples from the ends of the earth and other far-flung places converged on Jerusalem in fulfillment of a 30-year prophecy by a Pacific Islands prophet, Rev. Michael Maeliau. Their purpose was to return with the Gospel to Jerusalem in thanks for its having reached the farthest places of the earth; to celebrate the Glory of the Lord covering the whole earth and returning to Jerusalem; and to welcome the coming of the King of Glory.

Leaders of nations and tribes and peoples came bringing their gifts and their worship in honour of the King of Kings, bowing in humility. They came on the wings of the wind, the noise of their engines making a 'tumult'. (There was no vocabulary in Enoch's day for the planes he seems to have witnessed.) The Messianic Jewish community opened their arms to their Christian brothers and sisters, and the glory and holiness of God came down in awesome power. Significantly the holy convocation was led and hosted by the Israeli Messianic community (Jewish Christians), the 'elder brothers' whom the nations had come to honour. This Welcome the King of Glory event in 2017 was the first Christian conference the local believers had called, hosted and led since the rebirth of the nation of Israel in 1948.

The heavens noted it, the pillars of the earth moved. Reports stated, 'a huge shift took place in the heavenlies', 'Prophecy rolled out before us'.

The conference, unable to obtain a venue in Jerusalem, was hosted in Abu Gosh. City leaders, civic and spiritual, re-enacted their historic gateway role to Jerusalem by symbolically and prophetically opening the gates to Jerusalem.

Next day, on the 'last day of the Feast' (of Tabernacles), Jerusalem's closed doors suddenly swung open and the Glory from the East flowed in to the city for the climax and fulfilment of its destiny in its ordained place. The final day of the conference was held in Jerusalem.

Shortly afterwards the Messianic community gathered in Jerusalem to declare publicly that **Yeshua is the Messiah**.

And within a few weeks Jerusalem was acknowledged by the USA to be the official capital of Israel.[30]

Signs and preparations for His coming are happening with increased frequency.

See! the Lord is coming…! With thousands upon thousands of His holy ones who have been waiting for this day. They are joining us in this End scenario to finally drive out all wickedness, put an end to all evil and dissolve darkness forever.

In the next chapter we will see how this happens, and learn about the **Great Divide**.

---

[30] On Dec 6th 2017 President Trump formally recognized Jerusalem as the capital of Israel. The US Embassy was officially relocated to Jerusalem 6 months later on the 70th anniversary of Israel's Declaration of Independence.

THE GREAT DIVIDE

YHWH made a separation between the light and the darkness, and divided the spirits of men, and strengthened the spirits of the righteous. (En.41:8)

Enoch Defines 'the Righteous'

The righteous are believers who live holy and God-directed lives and have separated themselves from the ungodly practices of the world. They rally under His Name and are saved from the world's fate. Called 'Chosen Ones', **they** in fact have made the choice - to believe and obey Him. They give God great pleasure and He reveals Himself to them (a recurring theme).

- *The righteous allowed their deeds to be divinely orchestrated and completely dependent upon the Lord of Spirits* (En.38:2).

- *They have hated and rejected this world of unrighteousness, and have hated all its works and ways.*

- *In His Name they are saved, and their lives are lived in His great pleasure* (En.48:7).

- *The holy ones* (righteous) *believe in the Name of the Lord of Spirits forever* (En.43:4).

What the Prophet Ezekiel Says:

I gave them laws for living, showed them how to live well and obediently before me. I also gave them my weekly holy rest days, my 'sabaths', a kind of signpost erected between me and them to show them that I, God, am in the business of making them holy (Ez.20:11,12).

He describes *a person who 'lives well', treating others fairly, keeping good relationships, he*

> *doesn't eat at the pagan shrines,*
> *doesn't worship the popular idols,*
> *doesn't seduce a neighbour's spouse,*
> *doesn't indulge in casual sex,*
> *doesn't bully anyone,*
> *doesn't pile up bad debts,*

doesn't steal,

doesn't refuse food to the hungry,

doesn't refuse clothing to the ill-clad,

doesn't exploit the poor,

doesn't live by impulse and greed,

doesn't treat one person better than another,

But lives by my statutes and faithfully honours and obeys my laws. This person who lives upright and well shall live a full and true life. Decree of GOD, the Master (Ez.18:5-9).

As a result, *the Lord of Spirits has revealed Him* (Son of Man) *to the holy and righteous and He has protected the inheritance of the righteous* (En.48:7). Compare this with Jn.14:21 where the Son promises to reveal Himself to those who obey Him because they are the ones who love Him. Here is a God looking for relationship. This is a mutual choice. I think they're in love! After all He is coming back for a Bride.

What a Righteous Generation Looks Like

Clean

There will be a flurry of cleaning taking place for the return of the Bridegroom. The Bride is making herself ready. Holy Spirit is her assistant. The whole venue is getting a thorough cleansing in readiness for the Groom coming to move in with His Bride.[31] Heaven's hosts are coming to help in this final Earth clean-up, here is their brief:

> *Cleanse the earth from all the effects of oppression and from all unrighteousness and sin, and from all ungodliness. And purge the earth of all defilement. And the earth shall be cleansed from all impurity, and all punishment and torment, and I will never again allow these things upon it from generation to generation and forever* (En.10:20,21).[32]

Fearless and Trusting

Are you fearful of 'the end times'? The whole point of the new era is for you. It's like the days before the wedding. This is not an arranged or forced marriage; it's a love marriage – a mutual choice, I am yours and you are mine. The Bridegroom's focus is on you, and your radiant beauty. He's besotted with you; you can't do a thing wrong! And yours is the excitement of delighting Him and being with Him forever.

---

31 I have not found reference to the Bride or marriage concept in Enoch, but the clean-up and His moving in to live permanently with His Chosen Ones are repetitive themes.

32 This may be a reference to a millennial period – mankind is still multiplying generations on earth in a sinless environment. It may also link to week 10 of the Parable of Weeks, (see chapter 2) at the end of which comes *the great eternal judgment.*

You are blessed, Enoch says, to be ushering in this new era – an era of righteousness specifically for the righteous. Those days, just before the big day, are chaotic with preparations. The Lord gives fatherly promises to allay these fears and calm any nerves. One of my favourites is Nahum chapter 1:1-7

> *The Lord has His way in the whirlwind and in the storm, and the clouds are the dust of His feet... The Lord is good, a stronghold in the Day of Trouble, and He knows those who trust in Him.* [Read it in full for a courage boost.]

Enoch says, *I know that violence must increase on the earth, and a great chastisement be executed on the earth, and all unrighteousness comes to an end: yes, it shall be cut off from its roots, and its whole structure be destroyed* (En.91:5).

Confident and Powerful

Do You Worry about 'not measuring up'?

> *Let not your spirit be troubled... The Righteous One will give you power so that you shall be endowed* [gifted] *with goodness and righteousness and walk in eternal light* (En.92). *They* [the righteous] *will be as powerful as flaming lights,*

and their lips overflow with blessing... and righteousness will never falter [trip up, or flag] *in His Presence* (En.39:7).

What shall you be obliged to do? I love this. There's no 'To Do List' (except wait and hope). No works are required – just a few things to avoid. *You will **not** have to **hide** on the day of the Great Judgment; you will not be found to be sinners, and the eternal judgment will be far from you.*

> **Fear no**t, *when you see sinners growing strong and prospering in their ways.*
> **Be not** *companions with sinners.*
> **Keep far** *from their violence; because you shall become companions of the hosts of heaven*
> (En.104:4-6).

Expect increasing heavenly encounters, comings and goings through the veil.
Wait till an end is made of those who work evil, you who have done good; and an end of the might of transgressors.
Wait till sin has passed away (En.108:2).
Be hopeful; *for suddenly sinners shall perish before you, and you shall have authority over them* (En.96:1).

[Note: there are no preparation instructions, like 'build an Ark' to Noah. God **is** our Ark.)

Positive and Hope-Filled

Do you feel hopeless, victimized, want to opt out of life? Here's a conversation Enoch records (condensed). I'm sure you've heard similar.

> *"It's so hard and there are so few of us left - no help, no encouragement, no justice, no one to listen, no place to run. We'd hoped for reward, hoped to be the head but became the tail. We've been abused, dispersed, murdered and the wickedness concealed..."* (En.103:9-15).

God responds with a remedy in Chapter 104. "Here, take a few spoonsful of Hope:

- Angels record everything and remember.
- The gates of Heaven will open to you. [Note: in these last days there is a door open in Heaven and an invitation to come up (Rev.4:1).]
- Your cry for judgment will be answered
- and your tribulation will be visited on your oppressors."

Here are His instructions:
- Fear not,
- be full of hope,
- wait for the day when sinners are judged, for you will have goodness and great joy (En.104).

Good Times Ahead

Enoch keeps calling our focus to what lies ahead, keeping the end before us; "No matter the circumstances, don't lose sight of what's coming".[33]

> And there I saw the **mansions** of the elect and the mansions of the holy, and my eyes saw there all the sinners who deny the name of the Lord of Spirits being driven from there and being dragged off (En.41:2).

> When the day comes of the judgment and punishment for those who do not obey the righteous law, that day has been prepared for the elect as a day of **covenant** [fulfilment]; but for sinners as a day of inquisition (En.60:5,6).

> You are blessed you righteous and elect, because your **inheritance** is glorious. The righteous will live in the light… of eternal life; and the days of their life will never end, and the days of these holy people will be beyond comprehension. They

---

33 Compare Paul pressing toward the goal Christ Jesus (Phil.3:12-16).

will search for light and find righteousness in the Lord of Spirits[34]. *For there will be* **peace** *upon the righteous in the Name of the Eternal Lord.* The holy in heaven will even be told to look into the secrets of righteousness, which is 'the heritage of faith', for it has become as bright as the sun on the earth, and darkness is past (En. 58:1-6).

So here are the mansions John 14 talked about, and not an unbeliever left! This decisive day is the ancient covenant being fulfilled, and the righteous receiving their inheritance, the ultimate Promised Land. They sought after God and His righteousness and receive an indescribable place of unending light and peace.

'In Those Days'

Enoch was to pass on to us all the things he learned, so that we would understand what was happening in those last transition days. Here are some things to watch for:

A good period. *In those days, in the day of judgment, many and good days shall come to the righteous* (En.96:8). This looks as though the judgment of cleansing the earth will provide many good days for God's people.

---

34 So, seeking for Light is paid in righteousness, which is the currency of God's kingdom. See Abraham (Gal.3:6), for whose Faith God deposited righteousness in his account.

Your children will be saved. *In the **day of the tribulation of the sinners** your children shall mount up and rise as eagles, and higher than vultures will be your nest* (En.96:2). Note it's 'the tribulation of the sinners', not of the saints.

Expect extraordinary spiritual blessing and insight on your children.

A generation of righteous ones. Heaven's tablets read how evil will continue from one generation to another, ***until** a generation of righteousness arises, and evil and wickedness is destroyed and violence passes away from the earth, and all manner of good comes upon it* (En.107:1).

Expect an uprising of righteous anger against wickedness, and a growing purity movement as cleansing begins.

Houses of Prayer. *I saw the houses of holy people, that they lived alongside His righteous Angels. And they interceded and prayed for the children of men, and righteousness flowed from them like water, and mercy like fresh dew upon the earth* (En.39:4). Fickess says this is *"part of Enoch's blessing of our generation. I, [Fickess] believe he [Enoch] saw that our homes would become places of intercession where the angels of God would make their dwelling among us".*[35]

Expect the presence of angels, especially in house meetings, which will become watering holes for the community.

Ecclesia visible and unhampered. *The Chosen One will cause the house of His congregation to appear; from then on they will no longer be hindered in the name of the Lord of spirits.* (En.53:6)

Expect the True church to become obvious and operate without fear or inhibition.

Strategic Level Spiritual Warfare. *The righteous will arise from their sleep and be given wisdom* [strategies] *and they will root out the foundations of violence, and the structure of falsehood in it* (En.91 :10,11).

Expect revelatory strategies and extraordinary power upon God's people to destroy the very foundations of wickedness.

Defeat of wicked powers. *From that time on, those that exercise dominion over the earth will no longer be powerful and exalted. They will no longer be able to look at the faces of the holy ones because YHWH will cause His light to radiate from their faces* (En.38:4).

---

35 *Enoch's Blessings*, Michael Fickess, 2014.Morning Star Publications. P.107 (note).

Expect the downfall of wicked rulers.

Expect God to turn up the intensity of His light reflecting from you bringing fear and destruction of evil. (See also Is.61.)

Ungodly convicted. *In those days the righteous shall be a reproach to sinners and godless* (En.94 :11).

Expect unbelievers to react to the holiness of God in you; their spirits are being convicted and shamed.

Victorious Church. *In those days a **change** shall take place for the set-apart and chosen ones.* Light will be on them and honour will turn to them. They will be victorious in the Lord's Name and their lives will cause people to repent *and turn away from the works of their hands… and the Lord of spirits will have compassion on them, for his mercy is great.*

(These last-minute believers will receive no rewards but are saved by His enormous compassion. Enoch goes on to say:) *He is righteous in His Judgment, and in the presence of His glory, unrighteousness shall not stand but perish before Him* (En.50:1-4).

From henceforth *I will have no mercy on them* (v.5).

From that day *sin shall perish in darkness forever, and shall not be seen forevermore* (En.92:5).

Until this day *lasted the mercy and long suffering of God towards those who dwell on the earth… until the day of wrath* (En.60:5).[36]

This is the end point of Grace.

What Creation Teaches Us

God uses the meticulous order of His creation as a visual aid to teach us His ways.[37] From the beginning, the Creator set **functioning guidelines** for everything He created, to prevent chaos.[38] Not following these guidelines throws everything into confusion. God intervenes to prevent this.

Enoch had read in the heavenly tablets, details of mankind to the remotest generations. He saw the books already written before earth began. These laid out God's detailed plans for each soul He placed on earth. Enoch says: *I extolled YHWH for His patience with mankind* (En.81:3).

The Cosmic Oath and the Hidden Name

How everything operated, were important mysteries God revealed to His friend (En.69). The power that brought creation into being and the power which ran

---

36   Compare Methuselah's life, Chapter 1.
37   Compare 1Cor.10:11,12. All these things are for examples.
38   In *The Book of Heavenly Luminaries* (En.72-80) Enoch details the movements of the heavenly bodies finishing with a description of end-time chaos when *stars shall transgress the order prescribed.* See Chapter 4.

it all was the mystery oath. The oath was spoken with a Hidden Name. The Secret Name held everything together. *This oath is mighty over them* [created things] *and through it they are preserved.* He saw one like a Son of Man co-creating with the Ancient of Days and understood that the powerful oath was His Name. *And there was great joy among them, and they blessed and glorified and extolled because the name of that Son of Man had been revealed to them* (En.69:26). *The Word was with God in the beginning and the Word was God. Without Him nothing was made* (Jn.1:1-3).

He is Word

He is Truth

His word is absolute; it is Oath, inviolable,

foundation

of creation

By Him all

thingshold

coherence;

without Him

all breaks into

chaos[39] (Col.1:17)

---

39   Consider how drastically turning God's Truth into a lie would affect creation
     - or the effect widespread deception would have.

Watch

Watch the orbits of heavenly bodies [Again, Enoch instructs us to "see".] *(Watch) how they all rise and set in harmony, each one in its right season, because they never leave their fixed locations.* Earth and seasons, seas and rivers, clouds and rain, trees and fruit – *fulfil their purpose and never change their tasks.*

God speaks through all His creation. He made everything for a specific purpose. Everything that He has created operates in the same way from one year to the next. ***He is their true purpose, and these functions never change*** (En.chaps.2-5).

Enoch explains these things to Methuselah (En.72-79). He is impressed with how harmoniously and consistently everything works together, each faithfully following its set path and function, never diverting. Each star tracks in its own orbit, in perfect relationship with all around it. The sun and the moon follow the exact courses God laid out for them. All work together in perfect harmony and reflect their Creator's nature.

Reflection: Some of the heavenly bodies have their own light, and some are made to reflect light the way our moon reflects from the sun. Stars have their own light, whereas planets reflect light. But God Himself is the source of

Light and everything He makes is to reflect His glory and His divine character. He is the hub and focus of everything. Creation orbits around Him. We, His highest creation, are created to exactly portray His reflection, His image.

We are reflections of Him only if we face Him and orbit around Him, but if we lose our focus and veer off-course we create chaos. (Maybe we even create a black hole in the place where God created us to function!)

He directly likens us to the stars. *The Lord of spirits has showed you what they symbolize: they are the holy ones who dwell on earth and believe in the Name of the Lord of Spirits forever* (En.43:4).

I find it fascinating that the stars and all created things understood their specific function and the importance of keeping to the divine order and fulfilling their task.

I saw the chambers of the sun and moon which they come out from and return to, and their glorious setting, and their stately orbit, and how one is superior to the other, and they add nothing to their orbit and they take nothing from it, and they keep faith with each other, in accordance with the oath by which they are bound together (En.41:5).[40]

Enoch bursts into worship: *I continued to bless the Lord of Glory who has created all of these magnificent and awesome wonders,* **and he goes on to list**

God's Reasons for Creation:

- *to show the greatness of His work to the angels and to spirits and to men*
- *that they might appreciate His handiwork and all of His creation;*
- *that they might see how His creation demonstrates His infinite power*
- *and* **recognize** *this great work of His hands.*

  Note: God's passion is for us to recognize Him: *I'll do this,* or: *they were shown all these things… so that they'll recognize, acknowledge, know that I am God* (Ex.10:1,2 and many other scriptures[41]). This passion for us to acknowledge Him comes out of love; not His ego. Being out of harmony with His created order is harmful to us and those around us.

- *and shower affection on Him forever* (1En.36:4).

  Colossians and Romans also say this. *All things were created by Him and for Him* (Col 1:16). *For*

---

40 This could also refer to the law of gravity.
41 See De. 4:34; Ex.16:12; 39:46… all the way to Revelation.

since the creation of the world His invisible attributes are clearly seen, being understood by the things that are made, even His eternal power and Godhead, so that **men are without excuse** (Rom.1: 21).

He is saying, **creation understands Who God is.**

- *God has given understanding to everything that moves on the earth and in the sea – **yet sinners fear not the Most High*** (En.101:8,9)!

In contrast [to these inanimate things]

you have not been faithful. *You have not done what the Lord told you to do. You have turned away from Him and spoken proud and bitter words, speaking with impure mouths against God's greatness* (En.5:4).

Enoch is straight-talking. "Look at all these created things faithfully obeying God, **but You**, His prized creation and desired companion, you have not only disobeyed the Ruler of the Universe, but you have spoken arrogant hateful words about Him – with mouths that were created to praise Him."

God made a separation between the light and the darkness, and divided the spirits of men, and strengthened the spirits of the righteous (En.41:8).

THE GREAT DIVIDE

Enoch Defines 'the Wicked'

- *The people who have rejected the Lord of Spirits. It would be better for them if they had never been born* (En. 38:2).
- *They rejected the eternal heritage of their fathers* (En.99:14).
- Those who *deny the Name of the Lord of Spirits and His dwelling place* (En.45:1,2). [No God, no Heaven or Hell or after-life. Is this what your children are being taught at your school? Move them! Stand up for Truth and righteousness. Don't allow your children's spirits to be fed these poison lies. What their spirits eat is far more important than what goes in their lunch boxes! Bodies are temporal, spirits are eternal.]
- Leaders *who do not exalt and praise Him, or humbly acknowledge the source from which their authority was given* (En.46:5). *God has been angry with them because they do as if they were God* (En.68:4).

[Do your leaders act like little gods? God calls them wicked and is angry.]

- Those whose *thoughts shall err concerning the stars and take them to be gods[42]. Evil shall be multiplied upon them, and punishment shall come upon them so as to destroy all* (En 80:8).

[The heavens and the earth were made to declare God's glory. Astrology, witchcraft and sorcery are rooted in the kingdom of darkness which seeks to pervert God's purpose.]

What a Godless Generation Looks Like

The degeneration that occurs when people refuse to acknowledge God.

Depression. *The kings and the strong of the earth* [elite] *will become completely depressed through what they have made, for they shall have worked all their work in a lie* (En.48:8,9).

Fear/terrifying dreams. *Blinded through the fear of their hearts and through visions in their dreams* (En.99:8). Our young people are experiencing an epidemic of night-terrors and panic attacks.

Deception. *Sinners will alter and pervert the words of righteousness in many ways, and will speak wicked words, and lie, and practise great*

---

42   This could also include worship of celebrity stars.

deceits, and write books concerning their words (En.104:10). What a pervasive deception evolution theory has been.

Abuse. They *afflict the righteous* [innocent] (En.100:7). Devise wickedness, help oppression, slay their neighbours, deceive, abuse, spread malicious false rumours...(En.99:15).

Abortion. *And in those days the women shall become pregnant and abort their babies and cast them out. Yes, they shall abandon their children that are still sucklings and not return to them and shall have no pity on their loved ones* (En.99:5). *Fallen angels showed* [the women] *the wicked smitings of the embryo in the womb that it may pass away* (En.69:12). WHO estimates 125,000 intentional abortions are performed each day – 40-50 million per year.[43]

Perversion. On one of his journeys into the future Enoch cried out at what he saw, *"Woe, woe, how very terrible is this place". And those escorting me said to me: "This place, O Enoch, is prepared for those who dishonour God, who on earth practise sin against nature, **sodomy of a child**, corruption of children, and who boast* *of their wicked deeds: stealing, lies, slander, envy, resentment, fornication, murder, who are accursed and steal the souls of men, who, seeing the poverty of the poor, still take away their goods so they grow rich. This place is reserved for those who did not honour their creator, and instead* [indulge in] *unclean handiwork,*

Lawlessness and witchcraft. *Magic-making, enchantments and devilish witchcrafts* (2 En.10:2,3). Chapters 98, 99 describe blood-shed, drinking blood (vampirism), sex with angels, demons, animals, creatures, worship of impure spirits and demons (also En.7:5), and chapters 6-9, talk about secret knowledge, alchemy, cannibalism, slavery (human trafficking), human and child sacrifice... *In an instant shall they perish* (En.99:9).

Result. *Now their spirit is full of lust. They have denied YHWH… and believe not in His Name. The Judgment shall come upon them because they believe in the lust of their body and deny the Spirit of YHWH* (En.67:8). *This place is prepared for all these as an eternal inheritance* (2 En.10:3).

If you live a wicked life, you're guilty as charged

(Ezekiel 18:20).

Historic Interventions

There have been many God-interventions into history over the millennia to stop the chaos.

The Great Flood

Society had plunged into horrible depths since Adam had received his mandate to take dominion of the earth. Adam had sold out his birthright to the deceiving spirit inhabiting the snake and that spirit, the devil (Rev.20:2), had taken over the rulership. Looming before Enoch was the Great Flood. Life on earth had fallen into such wickedness and chaos it was slated for destruction.

Enoch prayed to have God-fearing descendants to the very End of time (En.84:5). God answered by choosing his great-grandson, Noah, to rescue from the Flood and start over. God's testimony of him was that Noah was *'perfect in his generations'*. Only those people and animals who responded to God and entered the Ark were saved. Everything else died.

Note: the animals came to Adam in the beginning to be named. They came to Noah before the Flood to be saved. Animals will sense God in you; they also are His creation.

Sodom and Gomorrah

and the cities of the Negev Plain were destroyed by fire from Heaven.

Abraham prayed and God answered by sending two angels to literally drag his nephew Lot and his family out of Sodom to safety. Even with angelic intervention his wife was in two minds about leaving. Her allegiance was with the city and she was destroyed with it.

Others

History is littered with days when God says **"ENOUGH!"**. Sometimes these are what are termed 'acts of God' disasters (as above), and sometimes God uses other instruments such as warring nations.

The end of Belshazzar's kingdom is an example, when Darius the Great overthrew him on the night God sent a supernatural hand to write on the wall (Dan. 5:24-31).

God still sends signs and warnings, and sends His prophets and His intercessors to plead with people (or with God on their behalf) - *'this most patient God, extravagant in love, always ready to cancel a catastrophe'* (Joel 2:13). See also the story of **Ninevah.**[44] It pains God that to rescue His creation from chaos He must destroy those **contaminated with evil.** Like a contagious disease, drastic measures are used to eradicate it before it infects the whole populace, and society is permanently affected – as we have just witnessed.

God promises to one day finally destroy the originator[45] of the rebellion and all who have been seduced into siding with him in the Great Divide. In the meantime, God works at getting our attention by sending warnings – physical and verbal.

'Turn, turn from your evil ways. For why would you die?' (Ez. 33:11).

Word to Noah's Day

Enoch was aware that God was about to bring judgment on the wickedness of the Days of Noah, his yet unborn grandson. Here's what he prophesied to them:

> *A command has gone out from the presence of YHWH concerning those who dwell on the earth, that their ruin is accomplished because they have learned all the secrets of the angels and*

---

44   Jonah ch.3.
45   See next chapter.

*all the violence of the satans and all their powers
and all the power of those who practise sorcery,
and the power of witchcraft, and the power
of those who make molten images. Because of
their sorceries which they have searched out and
learnt, the earth and those who dwell upon it
shall be destroyed* (Ch 65).

Word to Our Day

Double On the Way Enoch could see past Noah's
time and the flood that wiped it out, could see ahead
to the very end where wickedness was two times as
great (En.106:19). ('As it was' x 2!)

It was the righteous living then that he wanted to
address. Us! After all, it was Jesus Himself Who said,
*As it was in the Days of Noah so shall it be in the days
of the Son of Man* (Lk.17:26).

> *Unrighteousness shall again be consummated on
> the earth, and all the deeds of unrighteousness
> and of violence and transgression shall prevail
> in a twofold degree* [double]. *And when
> unrighteousness and all kinds of deeds increase,
> and apostacy and uncleanness increase,* **a great
> chastisement** *shall come from heaven upon all
> these* (En.91:6).

In other words when evil is over-the-top evil, a great punishment is coming.

God sends many prophets.

Jeremiah, the weeping prophet, pleads with hearers: *Look! I am preparing a disaster for you and devising a plan against you. SO, turn from your evil ways, each one of you, and reform your ways and your actions* (Jer.18:11NIV).

CHOOSE

Today there is still grace to choose,
but a choice is essential.
'Now choose Life. The Lord is your life. Listen to His voice and hold fast to Him' (Deut. 30:19,20).

In the next chapters we'll take a look at the mystery of Origins - how things came to be how they are – and the Omega – the culmination event where God presses the ultimate restart and the long-awaited Future begins.

The Divide

Choose today whom you will serve.

The righteous chose Him; the unrighteous rejected Him.

The Choice

Right	Wrong
Align with God	**Reject God**
Reward: inheritance, life	**Punishment: torment, death**
Enoch constantly contrasts the two sides:	
BUT all the righteous will be filled with joy and there will be forgiveness of sin and a manifestation of every kind of mercy and peace and patience (En.5:5b).	*The years of your destruction will be multiplied into damnation, and you will find no mercy* (En.5:5a).

See, the Lord is coming with 10,000s of His saints.

I Just Heard the Lion Roar!

It's November 2020 and I'm trying to finish this writing. I heard the Lion roar! This is track-stopping hold-your-breath stuff.

I have heard Him once before – the first time He appeared (about 2013), basking in the gold rays of the setting sun on my lawn. He has shown up occasionally since, but I've never heard Him again - until now. This time was different; I just heard the roar.

It was the roar of a lion roused – incensed and protective - an unmistakably 'don't-mess-with-me' roar. He will gather His Own under Him and protect them. (He did this for me once – I'd never felt so safe.) He is coming to deal with stuff.

Here's what scripture says about the 'roar'.

Amos 3:7,8. *A lion has roared,*
> *who shall not fear? The Lord has spoken!*

> *Who can but prophesy? – See, great tumults* and disturbances are coming....

Hosea 11:10,11. *He will roar like a lion. When He roars his sons shall come trembling.*

Rev.10:1-7. (After the 6th Angel (ch.9) releases the plagues of the 6th Trumpet and the survivors don't repent.) A mighty angel clothed with a cloud, one foot on sea and one on land and a little book in his

hand, *cried with a loud voice **as when a lion roars***.
Then the angel lifted his
hand to heaven and declared,
"NO MORE DELAY! THERE SHALL BE TIME
NO LONGER!"

(When the 7ᵗʰ Angel is about to sound, the mystery of God will be finished.)
This is a warning sign because these things are already upon us.

Another sign! Today (June, 2021), as I prepare to enter this story into the manuscript, my Bible reading is Jer.25:23. This is not a coincidence! The Lion is still roaring His warning. He wants you to heed it.

> *The Lord will roar from on high; he will thunder from his holy dwelling and roar mightily against his land. He will shout like those who tread the grapes, shout against all who live on earth. The tumult will resound to the ends of the earth, for the Lord will bring charges against the nations; he will bring judgment on all mankind and put the wicked to the sword.*
>
> *This is what the Lord Almighty says: "Look! Disaster is spreading from nation to nation; a mighty storm is rising from the ends of the earth. At that time the slain of the Lord will be everywhere – from one end of the earth to the other."*

The Lion of the Tribe of Judah is on His way.

From Origin to Omega

$\mathcal{T}$here was a beginning to evil. There was a time when everything was 'good' and evil wasn't known.[46] A major theme of Enoch's writing is the origin of evil, its disastrous consequences, and the journey to its final eradication and the restoration of God's original intent.

It's the story of redemption by a very long-suffering God.

In this chapter we'll take a drone's-eye view of the birth of evil, its invasion of planet earth, and the disastrous consequences for humanity and the planet. We'll trek with a broken-hearted Father reaching out time and again to a prodigal family who mostly reject

---

46 God examined everything He had created and pronounced it 'good'. In Gen.1:31 he summarizes His creation saying it was 'very good'. See Ch.1.

His Love – through past, present and future to the Great Day of the Lord when God finally intervenes to put an end to rebellion and deliver His creation. The drone will land here and there to connect us to our own locations and help us get our bearings on the journey ahead. Hang on tight; this is a bumpy ride.

The Origin of Evil

Enoch spends a lot of words on the origins of evil. How did the creations of a holy God fall into such degradation? The source, he explains, is in the spirit realm. Some early Christian fathers objected to this and rejected Enoch's writings from the canon of scripture.[47]

> One of the great tragedies of the church is how much of the Spirit dimension it has ruled out of Christian faith. Generations of youth have turned to other sources to satisfy their hungry spirits. Today's society presents a tempting smorgasbord of spiritual offerings, but it is poison. Unfortunately, few any longer know that the only Door to God's limitless other realms and supply is through

47   See Fore Word.

His Son. God sacrificed His Son to mend our broken connection with Him. Jesus is the Door. Enoch knew Him, way back pre-Flood, as the One *through whose Name they shall be saved* (En.50:3).

It's important to God to clarify the coup that took the allegiance of a third of His angels, and which is still tirelessly active to thwart His dream of having a Family, and a Bride for His Son.

A Series of Coups

Lucifer was one of God's archangels, in charge of possibly the most significant activity of Heaven. He was the gloriously decorated and powerful worship leader of all heaven's hosts (Ez.28:12-19).

1st Coup – Lucifer Against Heaven

When Lucifer rose up saying, "I will be like the Most High – Who does He think He is?" – God took decisive action and expelled him and his followers from Heaven, clearing them from the Command Centre.

Here is God's account of Lucifer's first coup, recorded by Enoch:

And one from the order of angels, having turned away with the order that was under him, conceived an impossible thought, to place his throne higher than the clouds above the earth, that he might become equal in rank to my power. And I threw him out from the height with his angels, and he was flying in the air continuously (2 En.29:3,4).

An earthly parallel story occurred later, recorded in Numbers 16. Priests rose against the High Priest, saying: "We are as good as you, who do you think you are?" God showed clearly who Aaron was - His designated representative. Interestingly, fire destroyed the coup leaders, and Earth swallowed the rest of the rebels. See the parallel on the Day of the Lord (next chapter). God cleared Heaven of insurrection, but the rebellion continued.

Lucifer morphed into Satan, and became 'Prince of the powers of the air' (Ep.2:2), full of hatred and revenge.

2nd Coup – Lucifer Against Earth

When God created Adam like Himself, made him ruler of Earth, and established an intimate relationship with his human family, Satan's jealousy grew volcanic.

Ulterior motives, seduction and lies were totally unknown to Adam and Eve. 'Become as gods' was Satan's lure. His coup was successful and he took over dominion of Earth.

> *Adam gave the names to all things living on earth. And the Lord appointed him ruler over all, and subjected to him all things under his hands, and made them dull that they may be commanded of man, and be in subjection and obedience to him* (2 En.58:3).

God's account of creation in Enoch goes like this:

> *I created man from invisible, and I placed him on earth, honourable, great and glorious, and I appointed him as ruler to rule on earth and to have my wisdom, and there was none like him on earth of all my existing creatures. And I called his name Adam*[48]*, and showed him the two ways, the light and the darkness, and I told him: 'This is good, and that bad,' that I should learn whether he has love towards me, or hatred, that it be clear which in his race love me* (2 En.30:12-14).

---

48   The name Adam is derived from the word for Earth from which he was formed.

Adam's choice started the constant battle over allegiance - who to follow. "Who tells me what to do?" (Rom.6:16 explains that we are slaves of the one we choose to obey.)

God allowed Adam and Eve to continue in His original plan, to multiply and fill the Earth (but outside of The Garden). Meanwhile He patiently looked for those who would choose Love, and relationship with Him. Enoch's passion to walk with God like Adam had in the beginning, was a joy to God's heart.

3rd Coup – Lucifer Against the Human Family

But by the time of Enoch's generation Satan had played what he thought was a master hand. 200 of his angels formed a pact to do the unthinkable – take human wives and have human babies. These angels were spirit-beings expelled from Heaven. But they had sexual relations with women whose bodies housed eternal God-breathed spirits. The product was mixed DNA and the corruption of the human species. (Enoch spends chapters 6 -19 on these matters. I suggest you read them.)[49] God forbade the cross-breeding of different species. Satan's goal was

---

49 For scriptural references to this event see Gen.6:4; 2Pe. 2:4.

to corrupt and pervert the human blood line so that God could not fulfil His promise of a holy Saviour being born into the human family (Ge.3:15).

Consequence

Hybrid Babies, the Giants

And they (the women) *became pregnant and they bore great giants, whose height was 3000 ells.[50] They consumed everything that men had acquired, and when humanity could no longer sustain them, the giants turned against them and began to devour mankind,* [cannibals] *and to sin against other living creatures. The **Earth** cried out in accusation against these lawless ones* (En.7:2-4).[51]

Depravity increased to such a degree that the giants were devouring the human race and creating chaos and destruction all around them.

Archangels blow the whistle

God's Archangels (En.9) reported these acts to God: "*The whole earth is now filled with blood and unrighteousness. The Earth itself is reverberating with the sound of man's intense*

---

50 The precise measurement of the ancient ell is uncertain. Some scholars believe some of these beings could have reached 100's of feet tall, but in later generations those encountered in biblical records seem to have been something between 9 and 12 feet tall.

51 Compare Abel's blood crying from the ground (Gen.4), and the clamour of cries God responded to in Lot's time (Gen.18:21).

suffering, reaching even to the gates of heaven. You know everything before it happens, and You see these things and You have allowed them, so why have you not directed us to do anything for them?" (En.9:9-11). [Note: The Angels did not respond directly to the cries of the people, although their mission is to serve the righteous. They may intercede, but they only act when directed by God to do so.]

God Acts

The Great and Holy One responded to the angels' intercession and delegated four angels to specific assignments:

Uriel, go and tell Noah, "HIDE YOURSELF IN MY NAME!" - the end is approaching.

[The instruction is the same to us facing this End of the age.]

Teach him so that he may escape, and *his bloodline may be preserved for all the generations of the world.*

[God had found a man with an uncontaminated blood-line, 'perfect in his generations', and saved Noah from the Flood in order to start over with a pure human line.]

Raphael, bind the leader of the wicked angels and
bury him in darkness in the desert. He will be
thrown into the fire on the day of judgment.
And heal the earth, declare its curse will be
removed.

[This chapter (En.10) is a valuable resource for
spiritual warfare.]

Gabriel, deal with the children of mixed spirit-
human intercourse (the giants) and eradicate
the corrupted bloodline. Turn their violence
on each other till they exterminate themselves
– and have their parents (fallen angels) watch.

Michael, bind those angels who have had relations
with women (after they have watched their
beloved children destroy one another). Bind
them securely for 70 generations, until
the judgment that is forever and ever is
consummated (En.10:1-15).[52]

Initial Judgment

So we see that at the time of the Flood certain
judgments took place, but they were holding
measures until the Final Great Day of Judgment.

---

52 Note that the time frame for this punishment is variously described as 10,000
    years (En.18:16; 21:6), for 70 generations, until the day of their judgment,
    until the eternal judgment, until the end of all generations (10:12,13).

- The fornicating angels were bound
- their giant offspring were annihilated
- the spirits of the giants were confined to Earth, called evil spirits or demons (En.15:8-16:1).

- *a great punishment* **took place** *and the earth* [was] *cleansed from all impurity* (En.106:14).

These angels had been on earth producing their offspring for around 1000 years - since the time of Jared[53], whose name means 'descent', alluding to the time of their descent to earth. Imagine how many descendants 200 of them could have produced in a millennium! None of their offspring (giants) survived the slaughter and the Flood, although their spirits remained to roam the earth.

It seems however, that further contamination occurred again after the Flood. Genesis records, *The Nephilim were on Earth in those days (and also after this)* [talking about the Days of Noah] (Ge.6:4). Later, as the Israelites proceeded to take the Promised Land the Bible says that they encountered and killed giants

53 See En.6:6. Jared, Enoch's father, was born in 460AA (After Adam). From then to the Great Flood was approximately 1000 years. (See chart in Chapter 1)

recorded to be descendants of the Nephilim.[54] As late as David's time we still have records of battles with these peoples, Goliath of Gath being an Anakim, descendant of Nephilim (Nu.13:32,33) who fled from Joshua (Josh.11:21,22) to take refuge in Gaza.

It is predicted to be again 'like the days of Noah', in the time of the coming of the Son of Man (Mat.24:37). No doubt hybrid beings and contaminated blood lines will be part of the clean-up about to take place.[55]

A Plea from the Condemned

While 'worshipping the Lord of majesty' on one of his visits to Heaven, Enoch received a call from the Fallen Angels. Would he please intercede on their behalf for an opportunity to repent of their wickedness. *I saw visions of chastisement, and a voice came bidding me to tell the vision to the* [fallen] *sons of heaven, and reprimand them.*

Enoch met them in a place called Abelsjail, located close to Mt Hermon on the current Israeli-Lebanon

54 Nephilim is a biblical name for the offspring of fallen angels. Other Post-Flood references - De.2:10-12; Josh 14:12,15; Judges 1:20.

55 Current gene manipulation, use of harvested foetal parts, artificial intelligence, and satanic rituals are among things which may open portals to demonic contamination of human DNA or species.

border. The fallen ones had made their 'headquarters' there after their exile from Heaven (En.6:6). *And I began to speak the words of righteousness, and to reprimand the heavenly Watchers. "Your petition will not be granted you… From here on you shall not ascend into heaven again for all eternity, and in the bonds of the earth, the decree has gone forth to bind you, for all the days of the world"* (En.14). But they wrote their 'sorry note' and appeal anyway, and gave it to Enoch, at which Enoch was suddenly transported in the Spirit, on clouds and wind, into the Throne Room to present the petition before God. Enoch describes the place as terrifying and full of fire.

In God's response to their appeal, we are given understanding of:

The Origin of Evil Spirits

Go, say to the Watchers (fallen angels) *who sent you to intercede for them:*

> *"You have defiled yourselves with the blood of women and have sired children with flesh and blood…and have lusted after flesh and blood."*
> *Now these giants who have been produced from spirits and flesh…*
> **evil spirits have proceeded out of their bodies.**

Even though they were born of men, their seed is from the fallen angels, so now they will only be evil spirits and they will be called evil spirits... and be confined to the earth...

Beginning with the slaughter of the giants, the evil spirits that come from their flesh (that is, disembodied spirits) will rise up against the children of men and against women, because they proceeded from them. They will destroy, afflict, oppress, attack, do battle, and work destruction on the earth and cause trouble, and face no judgment

until the day of the consummation, *the great judgment, in which the age itself will be finished over the Watchers.*

Then the fallen angels and the godless will be completely terminated.

"This is the final judgment; your petition is denied" (En.14-16).

Evil spirits take on many different forms in order to defile mankind and deceive them into: making sacrifices to demons, magic, occult practices and 'worthless' knowledge. *And the wives of the angels who went astray will become tempting* [seductive] *spirits (or sirens)* (En.19:1,2).

On Hold - 'Reserved for Judgment'

Peter alludes to this judgment of fallen angels in the New Testament - how angels, sinners, and the righteous are held until just judgment is made for each of them.

IF God

- *did not spare the angels who sinned, but cast them down to hell and delivered them into chains of darkness, to be **reserved for judgment**,*
- *and did not spare the ancient world* [Noah, Sodom/Gomorrah], *making them an example to those who afterward would live ungodly,*
- and delivered righteous Lot (who tormented his righteous soul from day to day by seeing and hearing their lawless deeds) –

THEN the Lord knows how to

- deliver the godly out of temptations and to
- ***reserve*** *the unjust under punishment for the day of judgment, and especially those who walk according to the flesh in the lust of uncleanness, and despise authority. They are presumptuous, self-willed. They are not afraid to speak evil of dignitaries...* (2Pe.2) [Read the whole chapter!]

Enoch elaborates on others being held for judgment: fallen angels and their leader, departed saints, sinners, martyrs, all waiting for that day.

Azazel - co-leader of the 200 Fallen Angels, was held responsible for corrupting the earth with forbidden knowledge, including how to make and use weapons, metals, allurements as in adornments, cosmetics, charms, witchcraft, spells, magic, roots and plants (En.8-10).[56]

Men were created to continue pure and righteous; and death, which destroys everything, should not have taken hold of them, but through this knowledge they are perishing, and through this, power consumes them (En.69:11).

Bind Azazel hand and foot and cast him into the darkness: make an opening in the desert - which is in Dudael[57] - and cast him therein (En.8:1).

On the day of the great judgment he shall be cast into the fire.... The whole earth has been corrupted through the works that were taught by Azazel: **to him ascribe all sin** (En.2:8).[58]

Note: two separate judgments are discussed

---

56 Possibly relating to hallucinogenic drugs.

57 This may have relation to Baalbeck north of Mt. Hermon, but could be purely a spiritual portal without geographic location.

58 The scapegoat, onto which all Israel's sins were placed each Atonement Day and was then expelled into the desert to Azazel, makes reference to this judgment.

above – the immediate one at the time of the Flood and ultimate one of fire at the Great Judgment.

Other fallen angels – are in a restraining place on earth **for all the days of the world** (En.14:5). Iron chains of great weight were forged to bind the hosts of Azazel until, on that **great day**, Archangels *shall take hold of them and cast them into the burning furnace, that God may take vengeance on them for their unrighteousness in becoming subject to Satan and leading astray those who dwell on the earth* (En.54:5,6).

Others on hold:

There are others also awaiting the great judgment day.

In those days shall the Earth give back that which has been entrusted to it, and Sheol also shall give back that which it has received, and Hell shall give back that which it owes. For in those days the Elect One shall arise, and He shall choose the righteous and holy from among them: For the day has drawn nigh that they should be saved (En.51:1,2). So Earth, Sheol and Hell are all currently holding souls for a future judgment.

Martyrs - *In those days* (at that time) *the blood of the martyrs from the earth shall ascend before the*

Lord of Spirits. **Heaven** dwellers celebrate, because **the number of the righteous has been offered** [there will be no more sacrifice], their prayers have been answered and the Head of Days has opened the books to judge on behalf of the blood of the innocent. They will receive justice and their suffering will end (En.47).

Departed saints – *Fear not, you righteous who have died in hope, nor grieve that your soul has descended into Sheol, or that in your life your body fared not according to your goodness. But **wait** for the day of the judgment of sinners and for the day of chastisement* (En.102:4,5). *Your spirits shall live and rejoice, and not perish. Much good will be rewarded to you for your labours. Exceedingly more goodness and joy and glory are prepared for you, than the lot of the living* (En.103:1-4).

Departed sinners - *Woe to you sinners, when you have died, your souls will be made to descend into Sheol and they shall be wretched in their great tribulation. Into darkness and chains and a burning flame shall your spirits enter* (En.103:5-8). *Sinners who deny the Name of YHWH; they are preserved for the day of suffering and tribulation* (En.45:1,2).

Interim Prisons

The spiritual beings and departed souls described above are being held waiting *until the day they will be judged and until the appointed time when great judgment will come upon them* (En.22:4).

Enoch visits the several places where different categories of spirits wait and describes them in chapters 18-22, & 70. He also saw the final (permanent) places of punishment.

Place of souls of the dead. He went to a mountain where human souls were assembled after death. Dark hollow places formed separate compartments to divide categories of spirits waiting there.

The righteous were in a place containing a bright spring of water (En.22:9). Enoch was able to mingle here with the *first fathers and the righteous who from the beginning dwell,* awaiting the Day of the Lord and their release and reward (En.70).

Sinners were bound in another part in great anguish, awaiting their day of judgment and final punishment (En.22:10,11).

Place of seducing angels. *Beyond the abyss* [of fire] *I saw a chaotic place which had no firmament of the heaven above, and no firmly founded earth beneath it:*[59] *there was no water upon it, and no birds, but it was a waste and horrible place. The angel said: 'This place is the end of heaven and earth: it has become a prison for the stars [angels] of heaven which have transgressed the commandment of the Lord because they did not come forth at their appointed times. And He was wroth with them, and bound them till the time when their guilt should be consummated (even) for ten thousand years.* **Angels who have been intimate with women will remain here until the great judgment day** *when they will be judged and totally annihilated'*

(En.18:11-19:1; 21:1-7).

Permanent Prison

From there I went to another place, which was still more horrible than the former, and I saw a horrible thing: a great fire there which burnt and blazed, and the place was cleft [split] *as far as the abyss, being full of great descending columns of fire: neither its extent or magnitude could I see, nor could I conjecture. One of the holy angels who was with me, said to me: 'Enoch, why are you so frightened?' And I answered: 'Because of*

59 Sounds like a 'bottomless pit'.

*this fearful place, and the spectacle of pain'. And he said to me: 'This place is **the prison of the angels,** and here they will be imprisoned **for ever**'* (En.21:7-10). RPT?
God's ultimate dream is on pause with a long period of grace, until that day when each one is allocated their reward.

Omega – The End

The Great Day of the Lord

Ever since the Fall, creation has headed towards this Day. In Scripture it is variously called: *The Great Day, The Great and Terrible Day of the Lord, Day of Tribulation, Day of His Wrath, Day of Judgment, Day of Trouble, Second Coming, the Coming Day, Last days, Day of Visitation, Day of the Lord Jesus...*

A Day Like No Other

Enoch talks about the Day, the power, the punishment, and the judgment that the Lord of Spirits has prepared. He states who the Day is prepared for:

- those who worship not [obey not] the righteous law,
- those who deny the righteous judgment [refuse to believe their lives will be judged], and
- those who take His name in vain [belittle the Name of the Most High].
- *For the elect the day is a Covenant, but for sinners an Inquisition* (En.60:6).

It's the Day God comes through on His promises to His people.

Isaiah talks about this Day when God shows up:

Behold your God! Behold He comes with a strong hand and His arm shall rule for Him, behold His reward is with Him (Is.40:10).

The Ultimate Convergence and Clash of Realms

Light and dark, good and evil, God and Lucifer - finally face off once and for all. It's the Day that divides Past and Future, 'then' and 'to-come'. It's the 'Time-shall-be-no-more' moment. It's the Past, crashing through the gates into Eternal future. It's the End of everything - that ushers in the New Beginning.

On Earth armies are marching; nations are converging determined to exterminate opposition, subjugate and rule the world (Rev 16:14). Another coup is brewing to take over earth's dominion.[60]

The Cosmos too seems hijacked, order and direction kidnapped. Tumult and chaos are unleashed (Compare Is.24:17-20).

But on this climactic Day, the God of the universes steps in. He intervenes one last time to restore divine order. At the end of this Day all that's wrong has been forever destroyed. What's left is what is rightly aligned with Him and the Divine plan.

God's dream becomes.

From thenceforth there shall be nothing corruptible; for the Son of man has appeared and has seated himself on the throne (En.69:29; 2 En.64:7).

What Happens on 'That Day'?

Enoch 1 Describes the Day – a quick review of what he said in his first chapter.[61]

In the Day of Tribulation, when sinners and the godless are removed from the earth,

---

60   See Chapter 4.
61   Enoch's nutshell summary is presented in more detail in Chap 2.

- The Great Holy One comes out from His dwelling in the Heaven of heavens, walks on Earth and establishes His Throne on Mt Zion (v.3,4).
- He comes with great power[62] accompanied by His armies to judge everything and to destroy what is not of God [ungodly] (v.9).
- Everyone is convicted of their ungodliness [how unlike they are to the image of God they were made to reflect], and of their rebellion (v.9).
- Every elevated thing sinks low and melts before Him. Every living thing on earth (and fallen ones under it) quakes violently. The whole earth is torn apart and everything dies.[63]
- To those who love Him God gives peace, protection and help, and turns up the Light shining from them (v.8; also En.38:4,5).

Isaiah talks about the coming of the Day of the Lord in Chapter 13 (also ch.66:15,17). He talks about the tumultuous noise of the nations gathering, and the Lord coming with His hosts, bringing weapons of indignation to destroy the land and its sinners from

---

62   Compare Is.40:10.
63   Compare Nahum 1:2-6.

it. At the same time the stars, the sun and the moon switch off their light and earth is dark. *I will shake the heavens, and the earth will move out of her place in the day of [the Lord's] fierce anger. I will punish the world for its evil, and the wicked for their iniquity; I will halt the arrogance of the proud and I will lay low the haughtiness of the tyrants* (Is.13:4-13).

The Time Perspective

The problem for prophets and their interpreters is to get the timing clear.

Isaiah was directing this passage against Babylon at the time, and it has no doubt seen partial fulfilment in that Iraqi city. However, it is obvious that the prophecy has a significant future fulfilment on a cosmic stage and joins many others waiting to be fulfilled on That Day.

As we look to the far end of Enoch's telescope, events may appear to compress where, in fact, there are spaces of time between them. Is the Great Day a calendar day, or a period of time? We know it's at the end-point of an Age. Is there a thousand-year gap (as discussed in Rev.20) hidden in there somewhere before 'time shall be no more'? In what order do things take place? There are questions our finite (and Greek-trained) minds struggle with.

It is possible, in the spirit realm, for many things to happen which challenge our understanding. Time is a measure which sets boundaries and corrals in our realm. We are controlled by it. But God is outside of Time, and He controls it. Separate things in our understanding may be simultaneous to a timeless God – or millennia apart!

A personal story. As an example, I relate this personal experience where God let me glimpse how different things can be in His dimensions. I was transported in the spirit to a realm where I was a child playing in the pool of a fountain. Simultaneously I was under the spray of the fountain enjoying the shower. And at the same time, I was taking a refreshing drink at the fountain. In other words, I was enjoying Christ the Living Fountain in multidimensions. Then He lifted this child out of the Fountain, wrapped me in Light as in a towel, and I was instantly a Bride prepared for her Husband. This story is to illustrate the difficulty we have understanding sequences of prophesied events - because they may not even have a sequence! Past, Present and Future are converged in the Eternal One. This is the limitless realm to which He is calling us – the realm which He is preparing for us; and the realm for which He is preparing us.

The Present is a landmark, a division for us between Future and Past; and Past, landmarked with historic events, gives us a perspective on an amount of time gone by. But in Enoch's telescope, foretold Future events seem to accumulate in a two-dimensional jumble, like an ever-shifting kaleidoscope. Future appears all one, brought up close into immediacy; there's little measure of perspective. Paul says,

We don't yet see things clearly.
e're squinting in a fog, peering through a mist; but:
it won't be long before the sun shines bright and we see
it all.
Until that completeness, we have
3 things to do to lead us toward that consummation:
Trust steadily in God,
Hope unswervingly,
Love extravagantly!!
Pursue love.[64]

---

64   1Cor.13:12,13 Msg.

Everything Happens Suddenly

It would seem 'that day' comes suddenly with an element of unexpectedness. This is remarkable after all the warnings from a parade of prophets, and the increase of signs outside man's influence!

Enoch addresses sinners: *For you shall **suddenly** perish* (En.95:6).

Then believers: *Be hopeful, you righteous; for **suddenly** shall the sinners perish before you, and you shall have lordship over them* (En.96:1).

Quickly: Jesus Himself several times mentions 'quickly' - in fact, in Revelation seven times. To three of the seven churches in chapters 2 and 3 he says, "I will come to you quickly…" And twice again in the last chapter (22), He makes the same statement.

His parables carry the same sense of surprise – the home-owner who would have been prepared had he known when the thief would break in! (Lk.12:35-40) *The Son of Man is coming at an hour you do not expect.*

Suddenly God's people wake up! Chapter 91 suggests that God's people have been asleep while violence, blasphemy, apostasy and uncleanness have doubled on earth. Then **suddenly**:

- they wake and 'arise',
- wisdom is given to them

- to cut off the roots of unrighteousness and violence
- and to destroy its whole structure,
- along with the deception (En.91).

That's a challenging and powerful word to God's people. Not only is it possible for us to effect change in earth conditions, but God is waiting for us to rise up and receive from Him the strategies to do so.

Climate Change and Cosmic Chaos

It would seem that the productivity of earth is seriously affected by some kind of change which may be the result of a cosmic event that throws our solar system into disorder. After describing the seven continents (seven great islands – two in the mainland and five in the great sea (En.77:8)), Enoch goes on to describe conditions of cosmic chaos he sees coming, both on earth and in the heavens.

Earth. *In the days of the sinners the years will be shortened, and their seed will be tardy [late] on their lands and fields, and all things on the earth will alter, and not appear in their time. The rain will be kept back; the heaven will withhold [it]. And the fruits of the earth will be slow and not grow in their time, and the fruits of the trees will be held back from their time.*

Heavens. *And the moon will alter her order, and not appear at her time. And in those days the sun will be seen and he will journey in the evening on the extremity of the great chariot in the west and will shine more brightly than accords with the order of light. And many chiefs of the stars will transgress their normal order. And these will alter their orbits and tasks, and not appear at the seasons assigned to them. They will be altered from all their ways* (En. 80:2-7).[65]

Angels of punishment marching

Enoch saw armies of 'angels of punishment' marching, carrying scourges and chains of iron and bronze. He was told these were the fallen angels who had been chained until the Day of Consummation (En.10). They had been serving Satan, preparing the instruments by which the kings and the mighty of the earth would be destroyed (En.53:3). Now God was sending them to the beloved children they had sired with earth women. We saw in Chapter 4 how their offspring were giants and when the giants were killed at the Flood their spirits remained on earth as evil spirits. Now their parents are once again forced to

---

65   Compare Jude 12,13. Some commentators hold that this prophecy was fulfilled after the fall of the angels. But prior to the Flood there had never been rain, nor do we have historic record of such cosmic phenomena. Since the anchor phrase is in the days of the sinners, I take this to relate to the period around the Day of the Lord.

bring punishment to their children and this time to cast them into the abyss where their lives will end, and 'the time of their deceptions be over' (En.56:1-5).[66]

Battle on Earth

These angels of punishment then stir up a demonically-incited war in the Middle East which brings about unimaginable bloodshed. In the end God Himself intervenes. The provoking angels are chased out from their hiding places in the earth and gathered for judgment, *they shall be led off to the abyss of fire and torment forever* (En.10:13).

Enoch describes how the fallen angels, having just destroyed their own children, hurl themselves East and stir up 'a spirit of unrest' among the kings, arousing them from their thrones to war against God's people. However, these kings ultimately war against and decimate each other.

> *(The kings) break forth as lions from their lairs, and as hungry wolves among their flocks. And they go up and tread underfoot the land of His elect ones.* **But the city of my righteous will be**

66　See Chapter 4, Origin of evil spirits.

a hindrance to their horses.[67] *And the nations will begin to fight among themselves till there be no number to the corpses through their slaughter, and their punishment is fulfilled* (En.56:7).

The streams flow with their blood. For a man shall not withhold his hand from slaying his sons and his sons' sons, and his honoured brother: From dawn till sunset, they will slay one another. And the horse will walk up to the breast in the blood of sinners, and the chariot be submerged to its height (En.100). (Compare Rev.14:18-20.)

The culmination: Sheol itself enters the battle and devours the warring armies. *In those days Sheol will open its jaws, and they will be swallowed up and their destruction will be at an end; Sheol will devour the sinners in the presence of the elect* (En.56:5-57:3).

God's Angels enter the fray. *In those days the angels [God's] will descend into the secret places and gather together into one place all those who brought down sin [fallen angels], and the Most*

---

67 This may have both a geographic and a spiritual fulfilment. Jerusalem, protected by God, has been a rock of offence to its neighbours; and the spiritual City of God, the New Jerusalem, has the power to defeat and destroy the forces of darkness.

High will arise on that day of judgment to execute great judgment amongst sinners (En.100:5).

The Righteous Protected. Despite all the bloodshed it's not all doom and destruction. The next verse follows with a 'but'. This is all about delivering God's beloved children. He delegates a contingent of angels to care for and protect them throughout the turmoil.

BUT (v.6) *over all the righteous and holy, He will appoint guardians from amongst the holy angels to guard them as the apple of an eye, until He makes an end of all wickedness and all sin.*

And the children of the earth [unrighteous] *will see the wise in security, and will understand all the words of this book, and recognize that their riches will not be able to save them in the overthrow of their sins* (En.100:6,7).

In the midst of all the chaos and destruction, unbelievers, seeing believers secure in God's care, suddenly understand that God's word is true, and they can't buy their way out of the decision they made to reject Him.

God Takes His Seat

The Ancient One, the Head of Days, descends to inhabit the earth with goodness. He establishes His throne on the summit of a high mountain (En.25:3). *And then I saw One who had a Head of Days and his head was white like wool and with Him was **another being whose countenance had the appearance of a man**. The Lord of spirits has chosen Him, and His place is to have supremacy before the Lord of Spirits in perfection forever* (En.46:1,3*)*.

Son of Man Given the Throne

God's ultimate aim has been to highly exalt His Son, give Him a Name above every name to Whom all will bow (Phil.2:9-11), and make Him Judge over those who have judged, misjudged and condemned Him (2Tim.4:1).

> *My Elect One shall in those days sit on My throne for I have glorified Him* (En 51:3).[68]

Result: Earth dances with joy and angels rejoice at this (En.51:4), *and you mighty kings who dwell on the earth, you shall have to behold my Chosen One, how he sits on the throne of glory and judges* the fallen angels - whom they followed (En.55:4).

His Triumph with This Son of Man will undo the power of the strong, break the teeth of the

---

68   Compare Dan.7:9,13,14.

mighty, cast down kings from their thrones and put down kingdoms,

because they do not exalt the Name of the Lord of spirits or humbly acknowledge the source from which their authority was given (En.46:4,5), *for they have denied YHWH and His Messiah* (En.48:10).[69]

Everyone *will see and recognize that Son of Man sitting on the throne of his glory* and His Name will be known. All fall on their faces before Him and worship in pain and terror (En.62:9). Everyone will know Him.

His Role As Judge

When the Son of Man takes His seat on the Throne, He takes on His role as Judge of the living and the dead. Now we see a demonstration of righteous judgment. *Shall not the Judge of all the earth do right* (Gen.18:25)?

Resurrection

The dead stand before Him Who IS the Resurrection and Life. No hiding in denial - ideas of oblivion after death!

---

69   See 2 Thes.1:7-10 The Lord Jesus is revealed from Heaven... in flaming fire taking vengeance on them that know not God and on those who do not obey the gospel of our Lord Jesus Christ.

Earth, Hell and Grave give back what they've kept in trust. They were the interim holding places, now they release their dead.

> *And He will choose the righteous and holy from among them, for the day has come for them to be saved* (En.51:1; 56:8).
>
> *Blessed is the man who dies in righteousness and goodness, concerning whom there is no book of unrighteousness written. Against him no day of judgment shall be found.*
>
> *But the sinners shall die with the sinners* (En.81:4,8).

Irrefutable records. *And the books of the living were opened before Him; and all His host which is in heaven above and His counsellors stood before Him* (En.47:3). *All things will be laid bare in the **weighing scales** and in the books, on the day of the great judgment* (En.52:15).

No lying in this court (En.62:9). *He shall judge the secret things, and none shall be able to utter a lying word before Him for He is the Chosen One before YHWH* (En.49:4). He is Truth, the awesome, holy, All-knowing One! It is impossible to lie before Him.

His Word slays. *The Word of his mouth slays all the sinners, and all the unrighteous are destroyed from before his face* (En.62:2).

Note: His word created in the beginning, and in the end, it slays what He did not create. Both *Life and death are in the power of the tongue* (Prov.18:21).

Sentences of the Wicked

The outcome of the judgment is that the Judge makes pronouncements on various manifestations of godlessness as His reasons for conviction. High on the list are:

> denying God's existence or authority,
> becoming servants of Satan, and
> leading others astray (En.54:6).

Although the unrighteous are judged individually, the ultimate sentence for each is expulsion from earth, from God's presence, and from the presence of His holy ones whose Light is unendurable to the unrighteous. They have nowhere to hide.

Michael removes *all that is wrong from the face of the earth* (En.10:15).

Just as straw burns up in the fire, so will they be consumed before the face of the holy (En.48:9).

And on the day of their punishment there shall be rest on the earth (En.48:10).

Omega - The End of What

At this point, as a new age of rest dawns for earth and its people, we see the end of many things besides the end of evil and unrighteousness.

End of Mercy. The opportunity for mercy is over; the door of the Ark is now closed. *Until this day lasted the Day of His mercy and long suffering, until the day of His wrath* (En.60:5). When the Elect One appears, there is no escape. *As wax before fire, they are powerless at His feet, none shall be saved* (En.52:6,7,9).

End of Earthly Kingdoms. Kings and the mighty are seized with anguish when they see the Son of Man sitting on the throne of His glory. They realize they trusted in their own power and grandeur. They fall down and worship, and beg for a chance to repent,

Confessing: "*Would that we had a respite to glorify and give thanks and confess our faith before His glory! But only darkness forever because we have not believed in Him nor glorified the name of the Lord of spirits, but our hope was in the sceptre of our kingdoms, and in our own glory. In the day of our suffering and tribulation He does not save and we find no respite for confession that our Lord is true in all His works, and in His justice. His judgments have no respect of persons. We pass away from before His face on account of our works, and all our sins are judged in comparison to righteousness"* (En.62 & 63).

There will be no other king but the Lord. *The kingdoms of this world have become the kingdoms of our Lord and of His Christ, and He shall reign forever and ever* (Rev 11:15)!

End of Unrighteousness. *Unrighteousness disappears like a shadow and will no longer be there. Because the Chosen One stands before the Lord of Spirits and His glory keeps increasing* (En.49:2). *All unrighteousness comes to an end: yes it will be cut off from its roots, and its whole structure be destroyed* (En.91:5).

And sin will perish in darkness forever, and will not be seen from that day forever (En.92:5).

End of Evil. Wickedness, anarchy, oppression, including 'mountains of hindrance' are removed once for all (En.53:1). *An end is made of those who work evil, and an end of the might of the transgressors* (En.108:2).

End of innocent bloodshed. *The number of the righteous was now offered and the blood of the righteous required before YHWH* (En.47:4). The limit to innocent bloodshed was reached. God said, "Enough!"

Rewards of the Righteous

The Judge examines the works of the holy and allocates rewards based on the weight of their **deeds** on the divine scales. Their **trust** in Him is also measured. Enoch talks about the weighing of the stars according to their light, this symbolizing God weighing His holy ones according to the understanding given to them. His judgments are received with great joy, and the 'Great and terrible Day of the Lord' ends with a glorious celebration.

Weighed. *The Lord of Spirits placed the Elect One on the throne of glory. He will judge all the works of the holy, and their deeds will be weighed in the balance. When he judges their secret ways, and their path according to the way of righteousness,* they rejoice, happy to be judged by a loving, righteous, and all-knowing Judge (En.61:8).

I saw how the actions of men are weighed in the balance (En.41:1).

Words, both righteous and unrighteous, the blessings and curses of lips, are also weighing in the scales at the judgment (En.52:15).

God calls the lightnings and stars of heaven by their names and they come. *And I (Enoch) saw how they are weighed in a righteous balance **according to how*** *much light they are given: I saw the width* [measure] *of their spaces and the day of their appearing, and how their spinning produces lightning: I saw how in their circling they rely on each other. They symbolize the holy who dwell on the earth and believe in the name of the Lord of Spirits* (En.43:1,2).

When some of the stars rise, they will become lightnings (En.44:1) This appears to indicate that some are permanently transformed into a high level of power and glory. *And all the righteous and chosen ones before Him will be as powerful as flaming lights* (En.39:7b).

Measured. Holy angels are given long cords to measure the faith of the righteous. Apparently the righteous may use these cords to stay themselves on the Name of the Lord, *and the chosen shall begin to dwell with the chosen* (En.61:1- 5).

Angels have a measure for faith – how much the righteous rely on the Name of the Lord of Spirits. It seems that the more they allow their deeds to be initiated by Him, the more holy ones dwell with them. My interpretation: In other words, the more we depend on the Lord and not ourselves (or others), the more likely we are to have angels living with and interacting with us.[70] (See En.39:4,5)

---

70 This however, may also be speaking about the necessity for strong bonds with those of like faith.

Rewarded

Angels have been assigned to record every detail of your life. The treasured photos and mementos you have gathered of your little ones, are nothing in comparison with what your doting Heavenly Father has kept about each little step of your journey. He has noted each kindness and sacrifice you made for others secretly, never expecting a thankyou. He's recorded the things you've borne in silence, He knows every wound and scar you bravely carried alone, and the pain you refused to let cripple you. You haven't worked for earthly gain, but have spent yourself building invisible wealth, heavenly riches. God's accounting and reward system will astound you with its astronomical returns!

Enoch read Heaven's books recording the stories of the humble, and those who afflicted their bodies [with fasting], those who were put to shame by wicked men, those who love Elohim and loved neither gold nor silver nor the good things in the world, but gave over their bodies to torture and martyrdom. Those who longed not for earthly food, but lived regarding everything as a passing breath. YHWH tried them much, and their spirits were found pure (En.108:7-10). Peter says, *Think it*

not strange concerning the fiery trial sent to try you...
When His glory is revealed you will share in it
(1Pe 4:12,13).

The Rewards. *They loved heaven more than their life
in the world, so He has assigned them their reward.
Though they were trodden under foot of wicked men,
and experienced abuse and reviling and were put to
shame,* **yet** *they blessed Me.*

The blessings destined for them: *Therefore I will*
- *bring them forth in shining light*
- *and I will seat each on the throne of his honour*
- *And they shall be resplendent* (En108:7-15).
- All kinds of good, joy and glory will be given to them for their labours.
- Their lot is abundantly beyond the lot of the living.
- Their spirits will live and rejoice, and will not perish (En.103:3,4).

Eternal inheritance. For the righteous who *endure
all manner of offence from those who exasperate
their souls, who avert their eyes from iniquity,
make righteous judgment, give bread to the
hungering, cover the naked with clothing, raise
up the fallen, help the injured orphans, walk*

without fault before the face of the Lord, and serve Him alone –

- a place of eternal inheritance is prepared (2 En.9).

This is a permanent dwelling, an eternal home. No more tents pitched some place in the wilderness, only to pack up and move on again. This is a priceless incontestable forever inheritance willed to you by name. It comes with a mansion (see En.41:2 and Is.32:17,18) architect-designed specifically for you, the beneficiary. Your reward is absolute stability forever in the arms of Love.

The Final Anthem

Worship ushers in the new era. The grand finalé, the Omega of the Day of the Lord, is an exuberant celebration. All from across the universe who have survived the Day are gathered - a host no man can number.

God will summon
all the host of the Heavens,
all the Holy Ones, and the Cherubim,
the Seraphim and the Ophannim,
the Angels of power and of principalities,
the Elect One
and the Powers on the earth and over the water,

and all the Elect who dwell in the Garden of Life,
and every spirit of Light who is able –
to Bless, Glorify, Extol and Hallow His blessed Name.
On that day they raise one voice,
and exalt in the seven spirits of God saying:
"Blessed is He. May the name of the Lord of Spirits
be blessed for ever and ever."
And all flesh shall beyond measure
Glorify and Bless His Name for ever and ever.
For great is the mercy of the Lord of Spirits,
and He is long-suffering (En.61:10-13).

So, the great Day of the Lord, The Day of Tribulation,
End Times, the Last Days, comes to pass

– ends –

in a burst of Glory that ushers in

the Here-after.

We are not finished;
we are still **here after** all of the tumult of that Day.
Over the threshold of this door is Eternity – forever.

Come on in.

After 'THE END'

He destined me for blessing and glory...
In Him there are no limits... (En.39:9).

'In Him' is a spiritual place which we are invited to enter in this life, but After the End there are no more limits; we are in Him Who fills everything throughout every dimension. There is nowhere where He isn't. We are in limitless realms - infinity. This is God's dream, to have His sons with Him co-ruling, and probably co-creating, the cosmos - Father with His sons enjoying the family He created for His pleasure. *And for His pleasure they are created. You are worthy oh Lord* (Rev 4:11).

Chapters 38 – 44 contain Enoch's descriptions of some of these other dimensions as God takes him on 'field-trips' into unknown territory, showing him what awaits after the end. He describes in 2 Enoch ten different 'heavens' and in most of them tries to describe the music – the 'formation of angel songs', the 'tongue of human song and life'. *I saw armed soldiers, serving YHWH with timpana and organs, with incessant, sweet voice, and various singing which it is impossible to describe and which astonishes every mind, so wonderful and marvellous is the singing of those angels (2 En.17:1). ...* Heavenly beings *continually with one voice singing one voice, and it is not possible to describe their singing, and they rejoice before YHWH at His footstool (2 En.19:3).*

Enoch tries to describe the many dimensions his journeys take him to. Sometimes they seem to overlap, or be fluid and changing. They seem to have no distinct boundaries and are therefore not clearly definable. These are the realms the righteous inherit after the end – unbounded time and space, and whatever other unimagined dimensions are in God's infinity. Be prepared for your mind and spirit to be stretched.

Extra-terrestrial Experiences Past and Present

Biblical Characters

Enoch was not the only one who experienced Inter-dimensional travel; it is not uncommon throughout our Scriptures. There are others recorded who visited cosmic realms, or travelled in supernatural ways. Enoch records many instances of being transported by angels, and being returned by them at the end of the assignment. Sometimes cloud or wind transported him. Once he describes being taken up in a whirlwind - like Elijah was.

Elijah's whirlwind journey however didn't have a return ticket. He is the only other human recorded who never died, but was taken directly to live with God as Enoch was.

Ezekiel was lifted up by the Spirit and taken all the way from southern Israel to the Jewish exiles in Babylon, Iraq (Ez.11:22-25). On another occasion a hand came and grabbed him by the hair and took him to Jerusalem (Ez.8:3)! He was taken on many involuntary journeys to other regions and nations, but none of his travel seems to have been galactic.

Paul wasn't sure if he was in his body or out of it when he was taken to the 3rd heaven, which he also calls Paradise (2Cor.12:1-4).[71]

The Apostle John was called to come up into a door in Heaven and immediately found himself before God's throne (Rev.4:1,2).

71   See En.32.

These were all involuntary experiences, not initiated by the traveller himself. God Himself brought them into other dimensions by various supernatural means, for His Own purposes.

Historical and Current Characters

Throughout history we have had saints leaving Earth realms on inter-galactic visits initiated by the Ruler of the universe.[72] It seems such interactions are becoming more frequent as we approach the End and the great cross-over of Ages. We hear reports of some being taken or sent on supernatural journeys which defy our natural understanding. Some on occasion experience power over physical matter the way Jesus did after His resurrection, when he passed through the wall into the room where His disciples were hiding. These stories often come from saints under life-threatening persecution where gates swing open as for Peter, or they become invisible as Jesus to the crowd attempting to kill Him. Brother Yun, *The Heavenly Man*, is an example.[73] Where God has a mission for his servant to fulfil, He can supersede Earth's laws on their behalf.

---

72 Springer R.R. Intra Muros "My Dream of Heaven". Book Searchers, Oregon; Guyon Jeanne. 1791. The Autobiography of Madame Guyon. Bibliotech Press, 2019; Sigmund Richard. 2004. My Time in Heaven. Whittaker House, PA

73 Brother Yun; Paul Hattaway (2002). The Heavenly Man. Lion Hudson

A Chinese Australian friend of ours was in Tiananmen Square on the day of the historic riots, preaching to students as bullets flew around them. Subsequently, foreigners were evacuated and further flights were cancelled. His frantic wife checked passenger lists on the last flights out of Beijing and he was not on them. Later that day she received a phone call. He had no idea how, but had found himself located in Hong Kong and was catching the next flight home.

Instances of people returning from death or near-death (NDE's) are increasing - just check the web! Many report visiting places beyond and unlike Earth. A number return from Heaven with messages about the after-life - warnings, instructions, encouragements, or insights into the future – because:

After-Life is an unavoidable part of our future.
You need to choose now where to spend it.
You don't need money for a deposit.
Just a passport stamped
With God-blood.[74]

Children

---

[74] God sacrificed His Son, Who carried His Own blood, to give us access as family to all His inheritance

There are many stories of children visiting Heaven; don't discourage them. Jesus said, *"Let the little children come to Me"*.[75] A missionary in China, H.A. Baker, Rolland Baker's grandfather, experienced an outpouring of the Holy Spirit on the children of their orphanage. The children were transported to Heaven, on occasions for many hours. They returned with detailed descriptions and messages. (H. A. Baker 1973 *Visions Beyond the Veil*. Whitaker House)

This is not an uncommon phenomenon and has happened collectively and individually in many societies. We ourselves experienced similar for a brief period in our orphanage in Bali, and Rolland and Heidi Baker's orphanages have experienced similar. There are a number of books of children who have come back from Heaven after a trauma. (A well-known story is Colton Burpos' *Heaven is for Real.*) These provide ever more description of life and places after the end.

God gives His people a taste of what lies ahead, sneak peeks of the glory and the expanse, and sometimes the terror. That these encounters appear to be happening more frequently I believe is a sign of the imminence of the cross-over for which all creation has been

---

75   An excellent resource work on this topic is Elizabeth Kotlowski's book 2007, Let the Children, Fireworks Publications, Singapore

groaning. Perhaps it's the Lord's urgency saying, "Get ready, the End and the After are upon you".

The Future: Earth and Eternity

After the Great Day, Enoch describes what seem to be two periods - one which is still measured by time, and another which is eternal – with no end. These seem to be two separate epochs, but it is sometimes difficult to distinguish either the time or place referred to - 'Millennial' or eternal; Heaven, Earth, or elsewhere! [76]

Earth

God's dream is fulfilled. Earth becomes what God originally intended. Its inhabitants live in perfect relationship with Him and with each other. They live fulfilling and productive lives, showing off His goodness and glory.

Enoch describes their lives.

The chosen ones:

- *will be filled with joy,*
- *and there will be forgiveness of sins*
- *and every kind of mercy and peace and patience.*

---

[76] The word millennium (a specific period of 1000 years) is not mentioned by name in Enoch, but this period of finite time without a stated number of years may be this concept.

- *Salvation will come to them as an exceedingly brilliant light*
- *And they will receive the whole Earth as their inheritance.*
- *Then there shall be bestowed upon the elect wisdom,*
- *And they will never again sin or disobey Him,*
- *nor die of the divine wrath,*
- *but they will complete the appointed number of the days of their life* (En.5:4-9).[77]

This then is a finite period in which days are counted and have an end.

Having, *at the great judgment* taken care of godlessness and uncleanness that polluted the earth (En 10:20), *He will bring everything to its eternal perfection* (En.25:4).

The righteous will be saved and they will live until they have thousands of children, and they will live in peace all of the days of their youth and their old age... free from the effects of oppression (En.10:17,20; 53:7). They will be allowed to eat from the Tree of Life and *because of this they will live a long life on earth just as your fathers lived* [pre-Flood] (En.25:6).

Earth Under Christ-Rule

---

77 Compare 1Cor.15:20-28. The last enemy to be put down is death.

There is One ruler, the Just, the Righteous, the Compassionate, Christ the King on His royal Throne. All creation is very happy.

In those days the Chosen One will sit on My throne... and the earth will rejoice - and the righteous will live on it, and the chosen walk on it (En.51:3-5). I will cause My Chosen One to live with those *who have called on My Name... And I will transform the heaven...and the earth and make it a blessing* (En.45:3-5).

The cleansed earth responds by producing prolifically. *Then the whole earth will be tilled in righteousness, and be planted with all desirable trees and vines and be full of blessing. The vine will yield abundant wine, and every measure of seed sown will produce a thousandfold, and every measure of olives will yield ten presses of oil. All the children of men will become righteous, and all nations will worship Me with offerings of praise and adoration. And the earth will be clean from all contamination and sin, and from punishment and torment. I will never again send these things on it from generation to generation for ever* (En.10:18-21).

So, during this period generations are still being born and people live longer (as in Enoch's time). Having eaten of the Tree of Life they complete a full productive life, fulfilling the lifespan allocated to them. This suggests that there is still death at the end of an allocated long life. People labour, planting and producing oil and wine. Nations gather peaceably and worship. Life continues on earth much as it was in the days of Adam before the Fall.

Old values destroyed. Enoch describes six mountains of metals - iron, copper, silver, gold, soft metal, and lead.[78]

And the angel said: "All these things will serve the dominion of His Anointed that He may be potent and mighty on the earth. In the presence of the Elect One they shall be like wax before the fire[79], and they shall become powerless at his feet. And there will be no iron for war, nor will breastplates or chainmail be worn. Bronze will be of no use, tin of no worth, nor lead wanted. All these things will be destroyed from the face of the earth at His appearing" (En.52).

Remember, it was the fallen angels who taught metallurgy to mankind - who used it inappropriately (c.f. En.69:6) and in service of other gods. The Holy One

---

78   It is interesting to note that millennia before scientists discovered the Periodic Table Enoch listed these metals in their precise order in the table of their nuclear fission/fusion capabilities.

79   Compare 2Pe.3:10-13 elements melt at His coming.

displays His supremacy over all these things which held power over mankind, including economic power.

*You are blessed you righteous and elect, because your inheritance is glorious. The righteous will live in the light of the sun and **their life will never end.** The days of these holy people will be beyond comprehension. Peace to the righteous in the name of the Eternal Lord! The heritage of faith has become bright as the sun **on Earth,** and darkness is gone* (Enoch 58:1-5).[80]

The Great Aeon

This appears to be an era distinct from the Earth period above. Now there is no measure of time forever, there is no toil or death and the saints have risen from the earth, no longer earth-bound. The Great Aeon comes after the Great Final Judgment when all evil and darkness is finally done away with. No more will there be 'afters' and 'untils', whens' and 'befores'; all these measures will have no place in measureless, boundless infinity.

When all creation visible and invisible shall end, and every man goes to the great judgment, then all time and years will end, and from then on there will be neither

---

80   These verses link to Earth, but mention eternal life. It does not necessarily mean, however, that the eternal life inherited is lived forever on Earth.

months nor days nor hours; they will run together and not be counted.

*There will be **one aeon (Age)**, and all the righteous who escape the Lord's great judgment, will be gathered in the great aeon and they will live eternally.*

*They will experience neither labour, nor sickness, nor humiliation, nor anxiety, nor need, nor violence, nor night, nor darkness, but great light. And they will have a great indestructible wall, and a **paradise** bright and incorruptible, for all corruptible* (mortal) *things will pass away[81], and there will be eternal life* (2 En.64:5-7).

'Glorification'

For this permanent residence the saints need to be appropriately clothed. Earth's flesh-coat is discarded and they are robed with the glorious garments of eternal life. *They will eat, lie down and rise up with the Son of Man for ever and ever. The righteous and chosen ones will have **risen from the earth**,[82] and been*

---

81 All things subject to death - things that decay, degenerate, degrade, decompose, destruct, disintegrate… Compare 2Cor 4:18 the things which are seen are temporal, but the things which are not seen are eternal.

82 As far as I can see this is Enoch's closest allusion to a rapture, but it's an oblique reference without a clear time anchor. It would appear to be after the Last Great Judgment, at the end of the perfect Earth period above. Of course, that Enoch doesn't mention something does not negate it. (It does prompt me to do a more thorough and open-minded study of Scripture which is my foundation.)

clothed with garments of glory - garments of life from Yahweh, and your garments will not grow old, nor your glory pass away before Him (En.62:13-16).[83]

Everyone will walk in His ways. Their dwelling place with Him will be their heritage, and they will not be separated from Him for ever and ever and ever. So there will be long life with the Son of Man, and the righteous will have peace and an upright path in the Lord's Name for ever and ever (En.71:16).

Paradise (*"How very sweet is this place."*)

When Enoch was taken up and placed on the 3rd heaven, he called it Paradise and described how God goes there periodically to rest. The glorious Tree of life is there: *I saw what this place produces and that it was so good that such has never been known. And I saw all the sweet-flowering trees and their sweet-smelling fruits, and all the foods that came from them bubbling with fragrant aromas.*

The Tree of Life. *In the middle of the trees was the Tree of Life, in that place* **where the Lord rests when he goes up into Paradise.** *This tree*

---

83   See 2En.22:8,9 for a description of when Enoch was so dressed and glorified, in the 10th heaven.

is of indescribable goodness and fragrance, and adorned more than anything else in existence. On every side it is either gold-looking or brilliant red, or fire-like and it spreads out over everything. It produces every kind of fruit. Its root is in **the garden at the earth's end.**

Paradise resides **between** *corruptibility and incorruptibility / spiritual and physical.*[84] [At the crossover point.]

Two springs come out flowing with honey and milk, and their springs send out oil and wine. They separate into four parts, and flow quietly in their courses, down into the Paradise of Eden, between corruptibility and incorruptibility. [Corruptibility is an impermanent, inconsistent realm subject to change and decay, in contrast to the unshakable realm of the changeless Eternal God]. *There they flow along the* **earth** *in their own cycle just as other elements. There is no unfruitful tree here, and every place is blessed.*

Three hundred very bright angels keep the garden, their sweet voices singing without ceasing as they serve the Lord every hour of every day.

---

84 Translations by Trimm and Lumpkin respectively.

And I said: "How very sweet is this place," and those men said to me: "This place, Enoch, is prepared for the righteous… for their eternal inheritance" (2 En.8-9:1).

So, Paradise is in (or is) the 3rd heaven and the Lord has a throne there, where He goes to rest, up in Paradise (En.32). It's the meeting point between visible and invisible, material and immaterial, tangible and without substance. It's the transition place, the cross-over point, between time and eternity, flesh and spirit.

Remember we are spirit-beings temporarily housed in a flesh body. This mortal flesh will be removed like Lazarus' grave-clothes and we will be freed into God's dimensions, where spirits are designed to live.

Garden of Eden

The Tree of Life which flourishes in Paradise is rooted in the Garden of Eden at Earth's end, and streams of sustenance flow from Paradise to the Garden watering the earth. The Tree of Life is in both realms, linking the two. The Garden at the end of the earth is also a cross-over meeting point of the two realms.

'End(s) of Earth', which Enoch often alludes to, is not a geographic location. Enoch encountered many such 'places' on his journeys, describing earthly geography enroute – mountain ranges, ravines, forests of aromatic trees, etc. But the ends of the earth are *where heaven meets earth and **the portal of heaven** is opened* (En.33:2). The Garden of Eden, sometimes called the Garden of Righteousness, or Paradise (En.32:3), is one such place.

Tree of Knowledge

On his journey to Paradise, Enoch arrived in the Garden with many glorious, fragrant trees *and then I saw the Tree of Knowledge. It is very beautiful. The fragrance of the tree penetrates the air for miles around. Raphael said, "your ancient father and mother who came before you ate of it and **their eyes were opened** and they knew they were naked and they were driven out of the garden"* (En.32). They were confronted with another dimension, one which God did not intend for them at that time. They knew only good and right; and by eating were plunged into a whole 'nother realm - of bad and wrong, sin and guilt.

Dimensions

God seems to be the initiator of Enoch's journeys into other dimensions, but he had a hunger to know God as his ancestor Adam had done, and a curious mind that kept asking questions about all he was shown. God promises that 'those who seek Me find Me', that He will reveal Himself to those who love Him (Jn 14:21).

Sometimes Enoch's journeys seemed to take the identical 'geographic' route with the same landmarks, but the end location was quite different. It seems the dimensions he entered are not fixed but fluid, revealing whatever God wants to show. Enoch encountered numbers of 'ends of earth' where Heaven meets Earth and the dimension changes to a new reality – where tangible merges into intangible, solid into immaterial. Here heavenly beings come in and out like on Jacob's ladder (Ge.28:10-17), which was a visual representation of a spiritual reality. Enoch found that God had provided many portals, or access points into His realms – communication or connection points with the Lord of Spirits. After all, that is what He longs for.

'After the end' portals will no longer be needed; everything will be open to the righteous. *In Him there are no limits.* He will have moved in with His people; He with us and we with Him in a way we currently find hard to imagine.

Personal Portals

I'm sure you have been using portals, probably without knowing it. They are what bring you into

God's Presence and awareness of Him - sometimes places, sometimes an action, a sound, a stilling, an attitude, His word, or just the closed door of your 'prayer closet'. In the Old Testament God called for a lamb sacrifice to access His Presence. Prophets like Elisha and David called for music or worship to bring the atmosphere of Heaven and help them transition into a spiritual place. Then in the Cross, God Himself provided the sacrifice and made His Son the Door. Before His departure Jesus established 'the Lord's Supper' as a communion-point, an interface with Him.

> Personally, I find this commemoration a strong entry-point into His Presence – a stilling, spirit-refuelling point.

When Jesus' mortal body left Earth in the Ascension, He sent His Holy Spirit to connect us and facilitate our fellowship and friendship with the other members of the Godhead. Holy Spirit takes us into spiritual realms, revealing things to us.

John was 'in the Spirit on the Lord's day' when He had *The Revelation*.

Oral Roberts used to talk about a 'point of contact', something tangible which triggered the release of faith.

Find out what triggers you into God-awareness, what brings you close to Him, what lifts your spirit into dominance over your soul. Frequent these portals for ever more revelations of His Presence. Relish the times when you close the door on a silent empty house and whisper, "It's just You and me now, Jesus".

Times do happen, however, when He just floods in with no apparent signal or portal; He is hungry for this relationship. Of course, it's not that He comes and goes; He is always with us, in us, and we in Him. It's our awareness that waxes and wanes, so that sometimes He just overwhelms us to break through and get our attention. Cultivate your awareness of His constant Presence and the proximity of Heaven as you keep praying for His Kingdom to be manifest on earth. One day soon it will be literal as well as spiritual.

I am expecting an awareness of God and His Presence to flood the earth, an awe of God where people are suddenly confronted with the knowledge of Who He is – an awareness of the life-choices they've made about allegiance. Hopefully that moment will still offer grace to choose.

Enoch's Farewell

Enoch knew that the time for his permanent relocation to Heaven was imminent. His assignment was finished and his writing task complete. He calls the family. They have known of their father's commission and deadline. They've become used to his disappearing, sometimes for weeks on end. Methuselah had kept watch at his bedside on at least one occasion (2 En 38:3). They had learned not to search for him when he was bodily absent; he would return. But this was final.

Now my son Methuselah call to me all your brothers and gather to me all the [family] and the elders; for the Word calls me and the Spirit is poured out upon me, that I may talk to them and depart as is planned for me (En.91:1; 2.57:1).

They've been expecting this. *All the blessings destined for them I have recounted in the books and [God] has assigned them their reward* (En.108:10), he had written.

The crowd gathers for this strange funeral and he addresses them. *My children, the day of my allotted term has arrived. The angels sent to escort me are standing here waiting. Tomorrow I go up to heaven, to my eternal inheritance. Therefore, I bid you, before YHWH's face, to do His good pleasure.* (2En.55:1-4) (Which of course we were created for.)

Listen to me my children today. He does a quick summary of the creation story, pointing out that

God created man after all the beasts and brought them to Adam to name and to rule, for men have a special place. As every soul of man is according to number, similarly beasts which YHWH created, some of which will also appear at the Great Judgment (2 En.58:1-7).

It is good to go morning, midday and evening into YHWH's presence for the glory of your creator. Because every breathing thing glorifies him and every creature visible and invisible returns him praise (2 En.51:5,6).

(He repeats two predominant themes here: learn from nature, and worship God.)

His Final Counsels:

Hear you sons of Enoch, all the words of your father and listen carefully to the words of my mouth, **which are all come to you from YHWH's lips** (2 En.47:1).

Before conception every soul already has a measure fixed of how much he should be tried in this world (2 En.49:4), *therefore my children, in patience and meekness spend your days. Endure for the sake of YHWH every wound, every evil word and attack. Requite them not because YHWH will be your avenger* (2 En.50:3).

I exhort you beloved:

- *Seek and* **choose for yourselves righteousness** *and a set-apart life* (En.94:1).

- *Love uprightness and walk in it, not with a double heart, but walk in uprightness my sons. It will guide you on good paths and righteousness will be your companion* (En.91:1-4).
- *Bow down to [nothing but] the true God. Walk before His face with terror and trembling and serve Him alone… whether in* (adversity:) *illness, abuse, provocation, wounds, temptation, nakedness, privation;*
- *walk children, in long-suffering, in meekness, in honesty, in faith, in reliance on promises, loving one another, till you go out from this age of ills, to become* **inheritors of endless time** (2 En.66:2,7).
- *Keep far from violence and walk in the ways of peace.*
- *Hold fast my words in the thoughts of your hearts and do not allow them to be erased, for I know that sinners will tempt men evilly* (En.94:1-5).

His Final Commission and Blessing

YHWH bids the righteous to: summon and testify to the children of earth concerning their wisdom:
Show it to them, for you are their guides and leaders over the whole earth (En.105:1).

This is his prophetic message to his righteous descendants at this end of earth's timeline: You have received this wisdom, now show and testify about it to the children of earth, because you are their spiritual leaders and guides. (Compare Jesus' commission to the disciples (Mat.16:18-20).)

Blessing

The service concludes with his blessing, both to his gathered family and to his family at our end:

In those days,
Blessed are all they who accept these words of wisdom,
and observe the paths of the Most High
and walk in the path of His righteousness,
and become not godless with the godless.
They shall be saved (En.99:10).
Blessed are the just who shall escape the great
judgment,
for they shall shine forth more than the sun
(2 En.66:8).

This blessing from the early Patriarchs to the generation that will complete earth's history, like the Gospel, is **Good News.**

Yes, it will get chaotic when God finally starts eradicating all evil – *when wickedness reaches its limit* (Joel 3:13), and God's grace comes to an end. Things will get shaky, but God is unshakable. You are in God; He is your Ark – your safe place.

So, for the joy set before you, endure through the End (it's just a transition) - the pain or the shame or whatever you may have to go through. The other side is glorious beyond description.

Joye Knauf Alit

Thou whose almighty word
chaos and darkness heard
and took their flight,
give us the strength, we pray,
and on that dark'ning day
as we walk in your way
Let us be light![85]

---

85 This grand old hymn, the latter lines of which I have taken the liberty to adapt for the purposes of this book, was written by John Marriott, 1813.

A Childhood Vision

Two Stairways

I was eleven. My first vision impacted the direction of my life. As a child I used to secretly leave kisses on the mantle-piece for Jesus at Christmas. I'm grateful for parents who introduced me early to the reality of the love of Jesus and our Father.

The vision was of two stairways. There was a landing or entrance place in the middle. The upward stairway was narrow and went straight up into a gateway open into brilliant light. I was aware each step represented a day, and on each step was a church. Not many people were on the stairway, but they were quite purposefully, climbing towards the Light.

The other stairway, which went down from the landing, was wide and busy. Each step was a day and on each step was a pub and a dance hall. The people were focussed on having the best time on each step. At the bottom I saw the last step ended and there was nothing but a pit of blackness beyond it. I saw people coming down and without a glance hurtling off the last step into the darkness. One or two caught sight of what was ahead. They stopped in horror then turned back, to climb their way up again to the landing, to get on the upward staircase.

I was horrified to see people, totally oblivious, hurtling over the end like that. I cried out, "Lord please let me stand on the last step and warn people to look".

70+ years later God is answering this prayer. I have just been reminded of it. This book is standing on the last step saying, "Watch out! SEE what's ahead. Choose the right stairway. It's not too late to change direction."

Am I not pleased when they turn away from their ways and live? Repent! then sin will not be your downfall. Rid yourself of all the offenses you have committed, and get a new heart and a new spirit."

(Ez. 18:23,30,31 NIV)

Frances Ridley Havergal, was one of my heroes as I grew up. This grand anthem, ©1877, has been on replay through my spirit throughout the writing of this book. Sing it with me.

Who Is On the Lord's Side?

Who is on the Lord's side?
  Who will serve the King?
Who will be His helpers,
  Other lives to bring?
Who will leave the world's side?
  Who will face the foe?
Who is on the Lord's side?
  Who for Him will go?

By Thy grand redemption,
By Thy grace divine,
We are on the Lord's side;
Savior, we are Thine.

Jesus, Thou hast bought us,
  Not with gold or gem,
But with Thine own life-blood,
  For Thy diadem;
With Thy blessing filling
  Each who comes to Thee,
Thou hast made us willing,
  Thou hast made us free.

Fierce may be the conflict,
 Strong may be the foe,
But the King's own army
 None can overthrow.
Round His standard ranging
 Victory is secure,
For His truth unchanging
 Makes the triumph sure.

By Thy grand redemption,
By Thy grace divine,
We are on the Lord's side;
Savior, we are Thine.

Other Books by Joye Knauf Alit

Available at major Booksellers

Jurisdictions

Take Charge of the Sphere You Influence

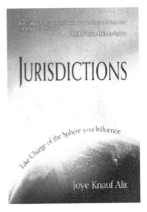

Did you ever dream of being a Prince, or Princess - or ever want to change the world? 'Jurisdictions' shows they were God-dreams; they are on His blueprint for your life. It shows how to align with His dreams and fulfil a destiny beyond your imagination.

Everyone has a jurisdiction. It is the sphere of influence God has given you over which to establish His dominion. Down-to-earth stories, personal spiritual encounters, and scriptures that burst with life help you discover and take charge of your jurisdiction.

This book is not just about taking spiritual authority. It will grow your confidence in the authority you have, its boundaries, and how and where to use it.

Jurisdictions confirms that the epic battle between Good and Evil does have a conclusion, and why your jurisdiction is significant. It provides instructions to fearlessly navigate your way, even through chaos, towards an unexpectedly delightful destination. God's dream comes true.

Milo Siilata, South Pacific

The Church, as the ruling council of God on earth, has failed to manifest the Kingdom of God. But with current events heralding the Day of the Lord, our understanding of our God-given jurisdiction has become critical for the Kingdom of God and our survival on earth.

Lynne Hamilton, Women's Apostolic Alliance

I'm so thrilled that this book has come into being. The church has great need of it. At this time in history the world expects that those who claim to belong to God will actually demonstrate His power and authority... Joye knows God in a powerful way. He confides in her - she is His friend, both qualified and authorized to represent His truth and His plans.

Heidi G. Baker, Iris Global

Joye brilliantly demonstrates how to have divine authority over our sphere of influence with informative, interesting and powerful insights into the dominion God has entrusted to us. Just as Jesus spoke to all forms of sin and evil, we too have a role in bringing the kingdom of God into our own jurisdiction.

About the Author

Joye Knauf Alit is a trained teacher, a professional editor and award-winning author. A long-term missionary (Bali, Indonesia) with linguistic training, she has pioneered orphanages, training school, foundations, churches, and cross-denominational ministers' fellowships. She has an interest in cultures, the more remote the better and has taught in Bible Colleges in some bizarre places, experiencing miracles, including the dead raised. She has been involved in global prayer movements, including the AD2000 Movement (for which she was *Prayer Link* editor), and the All Pacific Prayer Assembly.

Living with the New Zealand Maori during their spiritual revival of the 50's, heightened Joye's spiritual awareness and hunger. She has a passion to know God and walk with Him, and to help others release their spirit-being. She has observed how inseparably spirituality is integrated into most cultures, and how many incorporate a war between good and evil (with an ultimate climax or apocalypse) in their belief system.

To be asked to write on the Books of Enoch, however, was a surprise. "Write and make this ancient wisdom accessible to spiritually hungry people, especially your own Pacific-Asia cultures, and for non-academic people." It was a challenge to which Joye obediently dedicated two+ years of her life - listening to Enoch's heart, analysing, checking and seeking to understand his works clearly enough to present, as simply and accurately as possible, what he is saying. Enoch's passion was to walk with God like his ancestor Adam. One of only two men recorded who never died, he experienced enviable companionship with God, access into His realms, and unprecedented revelation. Joye's passion is to see people connect with God in a relationship as secure and mutually enjoyable as Enoch's.

Joye's 3 daughters, 7 grandchildren, and 1 great-grandchild are spread between Australia and New Zealand. When she is not consumed by a writing assignment, Joye is a vibrant 80+-year-old, plugged into the Source of Life. She is a God-carrier and a Joy-bringer.

Joye may be contacted at: joyealit@gmail.com

Her books are available from the above address, or from major booksellers.

9 780994 573629